1 MONTH

FREE

READING

at

www.ForgottenBooks.com

By purchasing this book you are eligible for one month membership to ForgottenBooks.com, giving you unlimited access to our entire collection of over 700,000 titles via our web site and mobile apps.

To claim your free month visit:

www.forgottenbooks.com/free601207

English
Français
Deutsche
Italiano
Español
Português

www.forgottenbooks.com

Mythology Photography **Fiction**
Fishing Christianity **Art** Cooking
Essays Buddhism Freemasonry
Medicine **Biology** Music **Ancient
Egypt** Evolution Carpentry Physics
Dance Geology **Mathematics** Fitness
Shakespeare **Folklore** Yoga Marketing
Confidence Immortality Biographies
Poetry **Psychology** Witchcraft
Electronics Chemistry History **Law**
Accounting **Philosophy** Anthropology
Alchemy Drama Quantum Mechanics
Atheism Sexual Health **Ancient History**
Entrepreneurship Languages Sport
Paleontology Needlework Islam
Metaphysics Investment Archaeology
Parenting Statistics Criminology
Motivational

ISBN 978-1-333-81164-8
PIBN 10601207

UNIVERSITY OF CALIFORNIA PUBLICATIONS

IN

PSYCHOLOGY

Vol. 1, No. 2, pp. 73-197, 6 text-figures   November 12, 1910

THE PROCESS OF ABSTRACTION

AN EXPERIMENTAL STUDY

BY

THOMAS VERNER MOORE.

CONTENTS.

INTRODUCTION.

The decade that is just now drawing to a close has witnessed a notable extension of the field of psychological research. In the beginnings of modern psychology the field of experiment was seldom extended beyond the domain of sensation. Progress in physics and physiology made it possible to subject our sensations to experiment, and for some time the sensory processes received the chief share of the attention of psychologists. It was not long, however, before the emotions began to receive their due amount of consideration and the invention of the plethysmograph opened the way to a new line of research. But only within the last ten years has the experimental study of such higher processes of thought, as abstraction, commenced to develop. The impetus to this new development has come mainly from Professor Oswald Külpe at the University of Würzburg. The present research, although its origins are not to be traced to the school of Würzburg, belongs to the field which Professor Külpe and his students have so admirably developed. Our problem was to study the mental processes involved in the formation of our abstract ideas. It is indeed true that the very existence of such ideas has been called in question. Still we may at present assume, for the purpose of stating our problem, that it is possible for the mind to perceive a series of objects, and to recognize some one quality or group of qualities as recurring constantly in every member of the series. The botanist examining a set of specimens will classify them according to certain characteristics which mark off the genera and species. The group of characteristics constitutes what may be termed his concept of the genus or species that he has segregated. Of each species he has a more or less definite "concept," by which he can represent to himself a number of specimens, no two of which are precisely the same. Such "concepts," whatever may be their real nature, are facts of conscious experience; we form them and use them incessantly. But what after all is the "concept"? What is the process of its formation? This is the problem of the present research.

The history of the problem dates back to the days of the Greek philosophy; but only within the last few years has it been subjected to an experimental investigation. The more recent literature is of immediate interest for our present problem. The metaphysical discussions, valuable as they are within their own sphere, bear only indirectly on the experimental question. Consequently, only the experimental literature bearing in some manner on the process of abstraction has been analyzed. Not every allusion in the extensive psychological literature of the day could be picked out, but a general account of the important pieces of experimental work from Galton to the present time has been given. The individual studies have been analyzed with some completeness because the history of the literature is an integral part of the evidence on one point of the present study, *viz.:* Is there or is there not a distinction between thought and imagery; and if so, in what sense is thought to be interpreted?

I.

LITERATURE OF THE PROBLEM.

The first experiments which in any way approached the domain of our abstract ideas were made by Francis Galton in 1878. In the *Proceedings of the Royal Institution of Great Britain* for 1879[1] was published his memoir on Generic Images. In this article he refers to an earlier one in the *Journal of the Anthropological Institute* for 1878.[2] The bearing of these experiments on abstraction is suggested rather than direct. But they have become the basis of the now famous composite-image theory of ideas, and are therefore deserving of mention. Galton described in this article the composite photographs which he had just succeeded in obtaining. These he compared to "our general impressions." Just what he meant by "our general impressions" is not clear; but he congratulates himself that his explanation coincides with that of Professor Huxley in his work on Hume. "I am rejoiced," he says, "to find that from a strictly physiological side this explanation is considered to be the true one by so high an authority, and that he has, quite independently of myself, adopted a view which I also entertained, and had hinted at in my first description of composite portraiture, though there was no occasion at that time to write more explicitly about it."[3]

Huxley's meaning is clearer, and to him we may turn for an outline of the theory. In the above-mentioned work on Hume, the following quotation gives a clear idea of the generic image theory of general concepts.

---

[1] Pp. 161-171.

[2] This article is mainly concerned with the technique of composite photographs.

[3] *Proceedings of the Royal Institution of Great Britain*, 9, 1879-1881, p. 166.

"Now when several complex impressions which are more or less different from one another—let us say that out of ten impressions in each, six are the same in all, and four are different from all the rest—are successively presented to the mind, it is easy to see what must be the nature of the result. The repetition of the six similar impressions will strengthen the six corresponding elements of the complex idea, which will therefore acquire greater vividness; while the four differing impressions of each will not only acquire no greater strength than they had at first, but in accordance with the law of association, they will appear at once, and will thus neutralize one another.

"This mental operation may be rendered comprehensible by considering what takes place in the formation of compound photographs—where the images of the faces of six sitters, for example, are each received on the same photographic plate for a sixth of the time requisite to take one portrait. The final result is that all those points in which the six faces agree are brought out strongly, while all those in which they differ are left vague; and thus what may be termed a generic portrait of the six, in contradiction to a specific portrait of any one, is produced. . . .

"The generic ideas which are formed from several similar, but not identical, complex experiences are what are commonly called *abstract* or *general* ideas; and Berkeley endeavored to prove that all general ideas are nothing but particular ideas annexed to a certain term which gives them a more extensive signification, and makes them recall, upon occasion, other individuals which are similar to them. Hume says that he regards this as 'one of the greatest and the most valuable discoveries that has been made of late years in the republic of letters,' and endeavors to confirm it in such a manner that it shall be 'put beyond all doubt and controversy.'

"I may venture to express a doubt whether he has succeeded in his object; but the subject is an abstruse one; and I must content myself with the remark, that though Berkeley's view appears to be largely applicable to such general ideas as are formed after language has been acquired, and to all the more abstract sort of conceptions, yet that general ideas of sensible objects may nevertheless be produced in the way indicated, and may exist independently of language.''[4]

·It would thus seem that Huxley's theory—and probably Galton's also—is that only our abstract ideas of *sensible* objects are to be compared with the composite photographs. Galton points out that the mind in forming its generic images is much less perfect in its mechanism than the camera. ''Our mental generic composites are rarely defined; they have that blur in excess which photographic composites have in a small degree and their background is crowded with faint and incongruous imagery. The exceptional effects are not overmastered, as they are in the photographic composites, by the large bulk of ordinary effects.''[5]

The experiments on composite photographs were not experiments on abstract ideas—they merely suggested a theory of general concepts. Nor did Galton's later experiments on mental imagery[6] approach very much nearer the problem. They called general attention to mental imagery and perhaps stimulated the next investigation of any importance[7] which was made by Ribot.

In October, 1891, M. Ribot published in the *Revue Philosophique*[8] his ''Enquête sur les idées générales.'' This he afterwards amplified in the fourth chapter of his book, *L'Evolution des idées générales.*[9] His problem was this: At the moment of thinking or reading or hearing a general term, what is there in consciousness—immediately and without reflection? On the basis of the imagery which his subjects reported he classified

---

[4] Huxley, *David Hume.* New York, 1879, pp. 92-94.

[5] *Loc. cit.,* p. 169.

[6] *Cf. Inquiries into Human Faculty,* 1883, Section on Mental Imagery.

[7] The article entitled ''Observations on General Terms,'' by S. E. Wiltse, in the *American Journal of Psychology,* 3, 1890, pp. 144-148, was only tentative and contained no definite results.

[8] Vol. 32, pp. 376-388.

[9] ·Paris, 1897.

them into: (1) The concrete type (visual or muscular imagery of an object). (2) Typographic visual type (visual image of the printed word). (3) Auditory type. A great many of his subjects said that they had nothing in mind. For example, fifty per cent. of the answers to the imagery of the word '*cause*' said that the subjects had represented to themselves nothing at all. M. Ribot then asked himself the question, What is this "nothing"? The word alone? No. Otherwise there would be no difference between a general term and a word of a language that one did not understand. The word is a sign of some object. We have learned the mental habit of designating many objects that have some point of agreement by this symbol. The objects designated lie hidden and are unconsciously represented by this general term. "General ideas are habits in the intellectual order." Our higher concepts consist of two elements—one clear and conscious, and this is always the word which may at times be accompanied by some shred of imagery. The other element is obscure and unconscious. M. Ribot refrains from saying precisely what this obscure and unconscious element is. From the context it would seem that he means the unconscious trace left by the habitual use of the word to designate various objects.

A word of criticism may be said in passing. M. Ribot's interpretation of this "nothing," which accompanies the perception of a general term, is purely theoretical and is not based on any published data given by his subjects. Furthermore, he has not followed out his sign theory to its logical consequences. For every sign, we have on the one hand the object signified and on the other, the signification. Smoke has on the one hand fire, of which it is a sign, and on the other a signification in the mind of the observer. If, then, general terms are signs, they have on the one hand the objects that they signify, and on the other a signification. This signification, as M. Ribot admits, is not the image and not the word itself. It certainly is not the unconscious factor he speaks of—for he would scarcely maintain that his subjects were not conscious of the meaning of the word. It is therefore a clearly conscious mental process distinct from both the image and the word.

M. Ribot's work comes closer to being an experimental study of the problem than Galton's experiments on composite photographs. Had he examined the state of mind of his subjects when they lacked imagery and not trusted to theory on that point, he would have carried his investigation into the heart of the problem of abstract ideas.

After Galton and Ribot the study of mental imagery took up no small portion of the time and labors of psychologists. But the extensive literature on imagery is not directly concerned with the problem of abstraction.

An excellent piece of work in this field of research is that of William Chandler Bagley of Cornell University.[10] He undertook to study the effect of imperfectly formed words on the perception of spoken sentences, and parts of sentences. The words and sentences were first recorded by a phonograph, the initial, middle, or final consonants being unpronounced. The subject listened to the phonograph, and was called upon to repeat what he heard, and analyze the mental processes he experienced. The section of the work which bears upon our problem is that entitled ''The Conscious Process Involved in the Apperception of Spoken Symbols.'' In comparison with the later German experiments, Dr. Bagley's are remarkable for the very frequent occurrence of imagery of one kind or another. His subjects in perceiving the meaning of sentences report with surprising frequence the presence of visual, auditory or kinesthetic imagery. This might be due to the fact that Dr. Bagley's subjects were capable of sharper introspection than the German psychologists. Still this can hardly be the case. The German psychologists, among whom are such men as Professor Külpe, cannot be supposed to be lacking in the power of introspection. Another possible explanation is that Bagley laid special stress upon the report about imagery and in that way developed in his subjects a ''task'' to associate definite images with the given sentences.

---

[10] ''The Apperception of the Spoken Sentence: a Study in the Psychology of Language.'' *American Journal of Psychology*, 12, 1900-01, pp. 80-134.

Though his subjects generally experienced imagery in the perception of the meaning of a sentence, still he finds cases in which this imagery is lacking. One factor which has to do with the lack of imagery is that "familiarity with the sentence sometimes militates against a clear and direct reference on the part of the observer." In this his results agree with those of Dr. Taylor reported below.[11] Bagley's general conclusion is that,

"The consciousness concomitant with the apperception of auditory symbols is made up of sensational and affective elements—some peripherally, some centrally aroused—in connections which vary in character with different individuals and under different conditions. These connections are arranged in patterns which change rapidly into one another, and are in general transitory and fleeting. When the attention is directed to the peripherally excited elements exclusively—when the external stimuli occupy the burning point of apperception—the meaning which they as symbols should convey is not clearly apperceived. When the attention is directed upon the centrally aroused ideas which the symbols suggest, the 'meaning' is apperceived, but errors and lapses in the stimuli are apt to pass unnoticed." (p. 125.)

He thinks that Stout goes too far in suggesting the existence of representative mental contents different from "visual, auditory, tactual, and other experiences." He thinks that his experiments lead him to no such conclusion. "From the series of observations which were made in the course of our experiments, no conscious 'stuff' was found which could not be classed as sensation or affection, when reduced to its ultimates by a rigid analysis. Neither do our experiments show that there is in the apperception of spoken sentences such a thing as 'imageless apprehension.'" (p. 126.)

Still Dr. Bagley finds something which he does not feel justified in putting down as either imagery or feeling. To this something which is not imagery or feeling and still has to

[11] See p. 87.

do with the understanding of the sentence, he applies the name 'mood.' ''We may say with Stout that the new is referred to a mental 'system,' in so far as such a system is a mood, an attitude, a tendency, an adaptation. The mind adjusts itself uniformly to uniform conditions: this seems to be the essence of the apperceptive 'mood.' When C, in the sentence ''The play was bad,'' interpreted 'play' as a drama, her mind adapted itself in a degree to the drama environment. This was not necessarily a focal reference to a given play, but the mind was in the dramatic 'mood.' Should particular parts of a typical play-environment have been ideally reproduced, the situation would only have been reinforced. Should certain verbal ideas such as 'drama,' 'theaters,' 'Shakespeare,' etc., have been reproduced in consciousness, either visually, auditorily or kinesthetically, these ideas would have been constituents of the dramatic 'mood,' but not necessarily the fundamental constituents. The fundamental constituents may and do vary from time to time. Only very seldom can they be called constant, and the 'constant supplements' which we have noticed are instances of such occasions. The fact that the focal constituents of the apperceptive consciousness are not necessarily consistent with the situation represented bears testimony to this point of view. ''There was not room for a stove in the corner''; with this sentence one observer imaged distinctly a stove in the corner of a small, otherwise bare room. His own surprise at the inconsistency of this imagery was shown by his exclamation upon recording the introspection: ''But there *was* a stove there!'' (p. 127.)

A 'mood,' therefore, is something that has to do with the past experience of the subject in regard to the words of the sentence that is understood. Just what it is, as a present psychical state, Dr. Bagley does not say. It is the revival of past experience. It is not mental imagery, although mental imagery enters in as a partial element in the complex termed 'mood.' If this is so, what is that present psychical state in the mood, which is neither imagery nor feeling? It is not past experience, for the past is not present. It is not revived imagery and feeling, for Dr. Bagley admits that the mood contains something besides imagery and feeling. It therefore seems that Dr. Bagley has found something more than he is willing fully to recognize. His experiments, like those of the later German writers, reveal the existence of an imageless mental content. Just what we call this is not of prime importance. But its existence should be recognized.

In 1901 appeared Marbe's[12] experimental study of judgment. His main problem is not that of the present work, but it is an early attempt to apply the experimental method to supra-sensuous mental processes. He also mentions, as a side issue, his attempt to develop the experiments of Ribot. The work was done in Professor Külpe's laboratory at the University of Würzburg, where Dr. Marbe was at the time Privatdozent of Philosophy. The method is essentially the same as that of the later Würzburg experiments which are described below. His final conclusion in regard to the judgment is that any special mental process—a word or gesture or image—may become a judgment. Taken literally, this conclusion is not borne out by the experiments. What they seem to prove is that a judgment may be signified by a variety of different processes. And this may be the author's meaning (cf. Chapter III). The perception of a judgment, however, is not a sensation or an image or a feeling, or anything that can be pointed out in consciousness. The perception of a judgment is a knowing—a ''Wissen'' (cf. p. 17).

In his concluding remarks on experimentation in the domain of logic Dr. Marbe mentions Ribot's work, *L'Evolution dés idées générales,* and refers to some similar experiments of his own on ideas and imagery. His meaning is not clear to me, so I quote entire the brief account of his work in this field (pp. 99-101).

''Seit den Zeiten des Sokrates hat man angenommen, daß den Begriffen im Bewusstsein ausser den zugehörigen Worten irgend etwas direkt entspreche, d. h., daß es neben diesen Worten

---

12 K. Marbe, *Experimentell-psychologische Untersuchungen über das Urteil.* Leipzig, 1901.

psychische Gebilde gäbe, welche der Gesamtheit der Gegenstände, auf welche sich die Worte beziehen, korrespondieren sollen. Diese Gebilde wurden ursprünglich, wie gelegentlich noch heute im Gegensatz zu den Worten, die nur Zeichen ihrer Bedeutungen sind, als Abbilder derselben aufgefasst, indem sie die gemeinschaftlichen *M*erkmale ihrer Gegenstände im Bilde enthalten sollten. Solche psychischen Gebilde hat man später je nach dem Grade der Abstraktheit, den man ihnen zuschrieb, bald als Gemeinbilder, bald als allgemeine Vorstellungen, bald als Begriffsvorstellungen bezeichnet. Obgleich, wie bekannt, ihre Existenz schon im Altertum und *M*ittelalter bestritten und in der Neuzeit hauptsächlich durch Berkeley bekämpft wurde, so hält man doch auch heute noch vielfach in der einen oder anderen Form an derselben fest. Auch die Frage, ob es solche psychologische Äquivalente der Begriffe giebt, ist eine rein psychologische, und ihre Behandlung sollte nicht, wie es in der Regel geschieht, mit logischen Untersuchungen vermischt werden. Die Aussagen unserer Versuchspersonen über die Bewusstseinsvorgänge, welche sie nach dem Erleben von Urteilsworten und Urteilssätzen zu *P*rotokoll gaben, enthalten übrigens nichts von solchen *P*arallelerscheinungen der Begriffe, ebensowenig, wie die wertvollen Untersuchungen von Ribot,[13] in welchen dieser Forscher einer Reihe von Beobachtern Substantiva zurief, um sich dann von ihnen sagen zu lassen, was die gehörten Worte für Erlebnisse auslösten. Ich selbst habe mehreren Beobachtern ca. 20 Substantiva zugerufen und mir dann von ihnen berichten lassen, was für Erlebnisse die zugerufenen Worte erzeugten. Dann gab ich denselben Beobachtern der Reihe nach verschiedene Karten in die Hand, auf welchen jeweils ein Substantivum aufgedruckt war, während sie nach einigen Augenblicken die Erlebnisse zu *P*rotokoll geben mussten, die durch den Anblick der gedruckten Worte in ihnen ausgelöst wurden. Endlich stellte ich ihnen die Aufgabe, die Begriffe: Baum, Volk, Gesellschaft, Zeit u. a. zu denken und mir dann die Resultate ihrer Bemühungen mitzuteilen. In allen diesen Fällen zeigten die *P*roto-

---

13 *L'Evolution des idées générales.* Paris, 1897, p. 127ff.

kolle nichts von Begriffsvorstellungen u. dergl. Die Erlebnisse der Beobachter bestanden vielmehr ausschliesslich in Wahrnehmungen, Vorstellungen und Bewusstseinslagen, die teilweise gefühlsbetont, teilweise ohne jeden Gefühlston verliefen. Man wird also wohl sagen dürfen, daß es keine psychologischen Äquivalente der Begriffe im Sinne der Begriffsvorstellungen giebt. Jedenfalls aber sehen wir leicht ein, daß auch diese Frage experimentell behandelt werden kann und muß und daß sie die Logik weiter nicht tangiert.''

The obscurity arises from the fact that it is not perfectly clear whether Marbe merely denies the existence of the general images which Bishop Berkeley[14] termed abstract ideas, or that he claims that there are neither general images nor universal concepts.

It would seem, however, that Marbe found no evidence for the existence of a general image in the understanding of the words given to his subjects. He did find, however, *Wahrnehmungen*, *Vorstellungen*, and *Bewusstseinslagen*. This latter is a term introduced by Mayer and Orth[15] to represent certain ''states of mind'' which are more or less refractory toward all

---

[14] ''Whether others have this wonderful faculty of abstracting their ideas, they can best tell; for myself I dare be confident I have it not. I find indeed I have indeed a faculty of imagining, or representing to myself, the ideas of those particular things I have perceived, and of variously compounding and dividing them. I can imagine a man with two heads, or the upper parts of a man joined to the body of a horse. I can consider the hand, the eye, the nose, each by itself or separated from the rest of the body. But then whatever hand or eye I imagine, it must have some particular shape and colour. Likewise, the idea of man that I frame to myself must be either of a white, or a black, or a tawny, a straight or a crooked, a tall or a low, or a middle-sized man. I can not by any effort of thought conceive the abstract idea described [in his previous account of the abstract ideas of the traditional logic]. And it is equally impossible for me to form the abstract idea of motion distinct from the moving, and which is neither swift nor slow, curvilinear nor rectilinear; and the like may be said of all other abstract general ideas whatsoever.'' *A Treatise concerning the Principles of Human Knowledge.* Introduction, 10, pp. 141-142, vol. I of Fraser's Oxford (1871) Edition of his Works.

It is evident from the context that Bishop Berkeley does not distinguish between the mental image and the abstract concept—between what is termed by the later Würzburg School the *Vorstellung* and the *Begriff.*

[15] ''Zur qualitativen Untersuchung der Association.'' *Zeitschrift für Psychologie und Physiologie*, 26, 1901, p. 6.

analysis—and in which images (*Vorstellungen*) are not to be found. In a later study[16] Dr. Orth attempted to show that the *Bewusstseinslage* was not a state of feeling.

That part of Dr. Narziss Ach's work *Über die Willenstätigkeit und das Denken*,[17] which refers to thought has a direct relation to this line of work, which we may consider as originating in Ribot's "Enquête sur les idées générales." The *Bewusstseinslage* of Marbe appears under the name of *Bewusstheit*. This author too has recognized the existence of mental states in which there "could not be detected any such phenomenal elements as visual, auditory, or kinesthetic sensations or memory pictures of such sensations which qualitatively determined the mental content reported as knowledge" (p. 210). There are often present along with such states of consciousness words or fragments of words. "Such a presence of kinesthetic or auditory kinesthetic images may well be the cause of the widely disseminated hypothesis that our thought continually takes place in an inner speech or adequate visual, acoustic, or similar kinds of memory images. Against such a view one must point to the fact that there are very complex contents in which, as already mentioned, the partial contents are consciously represented in their manifold opposing relations and still these individual contents are not expressed by any adequate vocal designations and the like—and indeed, it is absolutely impossible that they should be" (p. 215).

The question then arises, what are these imageless states of consciousness? This Dr. Ach explains by an example: "Every idea which is given in consciousness, for example, the word 'bell' puts, as is well known, a number of ideas in readiness, with which it stands in associative connections. This putting of ideas in readiness, or stimulation of tendencies to reproduction, suffices for the conscious representation of what we call

---

[16] Dr. Johannes Orth, *Gefühl und Bewusstseinslage.* Sammlung von Abhandlungen aus dem Gebiete der Pädagogischen Psychologie und Physiologie, edited by Ziegler and Ziehen. Vol. 6, No. 4. Berlin, 1903, *cf.* especially pp. 69-75.

[17] Göttingen, 1905.

'meaning' without its being necessary that the ideas should actually become conscious'' (p. 217). A nonsense syllable or a
word in an unknown language does not place in readiness any
such set of tendencies to reproduction and consequently has no
meaning. Every signification and every idea is an associative
abstraction because it picks out some of a vast number of possible associations. And no signification is identical with any
other but only more or less analogous.[18]

The problem of the understanding of words and sentences
was taken up by Dr. Clifton O. Taylor in 1906.[19] His first
experiment was based upon a similar one made by Marbe in
the ''Philosophischen Gesellschaft'' during the winter semester
of 1904, and may be considered as a continuation of Marbe's
line of work. He read to his subjects the following sentence:
''Imagine that in a rectangular space a plane is laid passing
through the upper and lower edges of two opposing sides. The
plane then must stretch obliquely through the space. How
many such planes can you imagine in this space?'' Then followed seven subordinate tasks based upon this fundamental
problem.

From the protocol obtained from his subjects it was evident,
that for the understanding of sentences expressed in concrete
terms the development of mental images can be useful, but
that they are not indispensable. These auxiliary images become less frequent the more familiar the subject is with the text.

A second experiment was carried out in which the subject
read a text from Gegenbauer's ''Anatomie.'' He had to take
care that he understood the text perfectly, and while reading
marked the places where he experienced any mental imagery.
Visual imagery aided materially in understanding the text.
But on writing out the text and then rereading the written copy,
the imagery was reduced from fourteen pictures to but one in
the third reading. On the other hand, from experiments with

---

[18] For a criticism of Dr. Ach's view see below, p. 181 ff.

[19] ''Ueber das Verstehen von Worten und Sätzen.'' *Zeitschrift für
Psychologie*, 40, 1906, pp. 225-251.

sentences composed of abstract terms, it seemed that the appearance of images hindered rather than helped the understanding of the text. With Taylor, as with other members of this school, the *Bewusstseinslage* comes into prominence, and it is found that these attitudes of consciousness are the *more* frequent as the subject is *less* familiar with his text.

We must now go back a few years to an independent line of research. Two years after the appearance of Marbe's experimental study of judgment, Binet published his brilliant *L'Étude expérimentale de l'intelligence.*[20] His experiments were commenced before the appearance of Marbe's work, for we read on page 76 of a series made in November, 1900. Binet may therefore be considered as a real pioneer in this field. He must too have exercised no little influence on later German authors, for he showed how the method of controlled introspection could give very valuable assistance in the study of our higher mental processes. He used in his experiments a variety of subjects, but most of all his two daughters, Marguerite fourteen years old, and Armande thirteen. His first experiment was to give them the task of writing twenty words—any that they might wish. By questioning he then found out in what sense the words had been used—and how they came to be thought of. By classification of the words used in repeated experiments *M.* Binet found very characteristic differences in the vocabularies of his two children. Their environment having always been the same, this difference, he concluded, was due to their temperaments. Temperament therefore has its influence on our choice of words. From the fact that the words written formed well-defined groups, *M.* Binet concluded that association alone does not entirely account for our train of thoughts. Association accounts for word after word in any group—but it does not account for the origin of a new group.

In another series of experiments the two little girls were given a word and instructed to tell their father of what they had thought. Binet was able to analyze this experiment into

[20] Paris, 1903.

the following stages: (1) The hearing of the word. (2) The perception of its sense. (3) An effort to call up an image or determine a thought. (4) The appearance of the image. One of the observations of Armande shows very clearly the distinction between stages two and three. "As yet there are no images (at the moment of choice) and I know why there are none: When there are many things such—for example, a house, there are many houses—it is necessary to choose. Just then I think about it without representing anything to myself as an image" (p. 75). Sometimes, however, says Binet, the image comes without being sought.

Binet gives a special chapter to the problem of thought without images. The conclusion at which he arrives is that neither visual imagery nor internal words, either alone or together, account for that complex mental process which we term thought. The grounds for this conclusion are the many instances in which his subjects had not and could not find any visual imagery for their thoughts. And again there were times when he thought that he could determine that word-imagery was also entirely lacking.

Binet also attempted, and with success, to have his little girls give a rating for the clearness of their images. These ratings ranged from 0 for very weak images up to 20 for images as clear and well defined as actual sensations of sight.

In Marguerite there were three well-defined groups:

I. A group in which the rating was usually 20, or a little below. This group contained memory images of well known objects or things recently seen.

II. A group in which the rating ranged from 10 to 15. This group contained memory images of objects not recently seen.

III. A group in which the rating ranged from 3 to 6. This contained memory images of things read or heard about and fictitious images of imagination.

With his other subject, Armande, the differences were not so clear. M. Binet gave up hope of finding any regularity. He published, however, the ratings for the three classes. The averages, which he did not give, are for Class I, 6.2; Class II, 4.9; Class III, 2.8. Considering that Armande's ratings ranged from 0-12, and Marguerite's from 0-20, one would not expect the classes to be so well defined. The ratings of Armande, however, show the same tendency as those of Marguerite—only not so marked. The small number of cases, however, leaves the result uncertain.

In his discussion of the theory of abstract thought and images *M*. Binet says that his data would support any theory. He makes this claim on the basis of a strange assumption that the discussions between nominalists and realists and conceptualists have always concerned images and not thoughts. He does not exactly state this assumption but it is evident from the text. He then comes to his *intentional* theory of the image. The image may be used by the person to represent a particular or general signification. It represents whatever the subject *intends* that it should. He would place, therefore, intentionism as a new theory alongside of realism, nominalism, and conceptualism. With Binet then there is thought, image, and object. The image is an arbitrary sign to which the subject gives at will a particular or general significance. In our mental life there are those distinct classes of phenomena—thought, image, and interior language. Association alone does not account for the mechanism of thought. It is more complex and supposes constantly such operations as choice and direction. The stream of thought is far wider and deeper than that of our imagery. The last sentence of the book is this: ''Finally—and this is the main fact, fruitful in consequences for the philosophers—the entire logic of thought escapes our imagery.''

The next experimental work on abstraction was that of Professor Külpe. A report of this was read at the German Psychological Congress, which met at Giessen in the summer of 1904. This was the beginning of a series of experimental studies by several of Külpe's students in his laboratory at Würzburg.

The first experiments of Professor Külpe were made in the

summer of 1900, with Professor Bryan of Indiana.[21] Külpe was not satisfied with these and decided to take up the problem again with improved methods. By means of a stereopticon lantern he projected upon a screen in a dark room the figures that were to be observed by the subject. The objects projected were nonsense syllables, four in number, which were grouped at equal distances around a given point of fixation. Each nonsense syllable consisted of a vowel and two consonants. The syllables might be in four different colors—red, green, purple, or black. In the different experiments also the four syllables were grouped so as to form various figures. A group of syllables forming with their different colors some kind of a figure was termed by Külpe an object. The subject could be instructed to observe the object from some definite point of view, or he could be left to observe the object without any prescribed task. There were four points of view given to his subjects:

1. The determination of the entire number of letters visible.

2. The determination of the colors and their approximate positions in the field of consciousness.

3. The determination of the figure which the grouping of the syllables formed.

4. The determination of as many letters as possible, with their positions in the field of vision.

The number of statements possible to any subject about the individual letters could be classified as follows: (*a*) The entire number of statements made; (*b*) the correct statements; (*c*) the incorrect; (*d*) the indeterminate statements; and (*e*) those that could have been made but were not. Each division could then be rated by its proper percentage of the entire number of statements. Where task and statement come together (*i.e.*, in the statements about the task) the percentage of correct (*b*) statements is a maximum and that of unmade (*e*), indeterminate (*d*), and in general also false (*c*) statements is a minimum. This

---

[21] O. Külpe, ''Versuche über Abstraktion.'' *Bericht über den I. Kongress für experimentelle Psychologie in Giessen, 1904.* Leipzig, 1904.

proves that "Abstraction in the sense of an accentuation of certain portions of a mental content, *i.e.*, positive abstraction, succeeds best when a preoccupation of consciousness—a predisposition for the partial content, is given or provided for." (*op. cit.*, p. 61.)

Negative abstraction—the tendency to neglect or forget all but the one thing abstracted—is the more complete the greater the difficulty of the task.

In explaining these results Külpe asks what is the reason for the effect of the task? "Were," he writes, "the *elements* or the *colors* seen differently under the influence of corresponding or heterogeneous tasks, or were they apprehended (*aufgefasst*) differently? . . . According to our protocol and the entire conditions of the experiment, to that question one can only answer that the difference lies merely, or at least chiefly, in the apprehension and not in the sensations" (p. 66). The task does not affect sensation but it does affect apperception. If that is so, then there must be a distinction between sensations and our perception of them. "That this distinction must be made in much the same sense in which we distinguish between physical phenomena and our consciousness of them; that, in other words, the old doctrine of an inner sense with the involved idea of a distinction between the reality of consciousness and objectivity must now have its opportune renewal in the domain of psychology—this is the principal result that I would draw from my experiments." (p. 67.)

Henry J. Watt, a student of Professor Külpe, published[22] in 1905 his ingenious attempt to approach the experimental treatment of the supra-sensuous mental processes by a study of reactions of association. As is well known, the reaction-time of association was originally measured by experiments in which the subject was instructed to respond to a given word with the first that occurred to his mind. Watt modified this form of procedure by limiting the freedom of the subject, setting

---

[22] "Experimentelle Beiträge zu einer Theorie des Denkens." *Archiv für die ges. Psychol.*, 4, 1905, pp. 289-436.

before him a more definite "task." He was to respond, not
with any word at all, but with a word that bore a certain kind
of relation to the word given as a stimulus. The subject had
six of these tasks, constituting six separate sets of experiments.
They were:

1. Seek a word under whose meaning the given word is
included.

2. Seek one which is included under the meaning of the
given word.

3. Seek the corresponding whole.

4. Seek a part.

5. Seek a coördinate idea.

6. Seek another part of the common whole.

All the words given were familiar nouns, nearly always
consisting of only two syllables, and never evidently compound
words. Five hundred such words were found and printed for
use in the various "tasks."

One of the principal objects of research in this study was
the influence of the "task" on the whole course of events in
a given experiment. In analyzing the results it appears that
there are two general classes into which the experiments may
be divided: (1) That in which the association is found by a
simple and direct process which suffers no disturbance in its
course. Verbal and visual images may be present but they help,
or at least do not hinder, the finding of the required association.
(2) The second class is that in which the development is complex. The subject tries two or more paths before he hits upon
the one that gives the desired result.

The first class of associations is subdivided according as
(*a*) visual images give rise to the association, or (*b*) a verbal
image or a group of verbal images, or a condition of recollection,
etc., or (*c*) no kind of imagery or media of association can be
determined to show how the word spoken was found.

In reproduction of complicated development one can point
to two subclasses: (*a*) The subject sought for something else,
or some other idea hung in his mind without his being able to

determine just what it was. (*b*) The subject sought after some more or less definitely determined idea, but could not find it; or he had something in mind, but for one reason or another rejected it.

One way in which the influence of the task manifested itself was the mode in which it determined the means of the association. Task 3 (whole), 4 (part), and 6 (part of the common whole) tend to increase the use of visual images. Task 2 (species) tends to increase the use of verbal images, and Task 5 (coördinate ideas) tends to do away with the use of both verbal and visual imagery.

Under the head of visual images Watt brings forward some interesting facts that bear in the main upon two important problems. One is the problem with which Berkeley found so much difficulty: Are all images definite and concrete, or is there any such thing as a general image? The introspection of his subjects seems to point to the existence of what is at least a very indefinite image. We quote some examples that he has given as typical: ''Hide: Image of an animal torso thickly covered with hair (very unclear). To what animal it belonged I do not know. Grain: Fleeting image of a rye or wheat field —the species was not clear. *M*outh (*Maul*): Beast. Dark image of an utterly undefinable animal. It could have been an ox, or a horse, or a dog with stronger definition of the head and mouth region.''[23] Watt calls attention to the fact that in this last case the image did function as if it were universal. One can, he says, maintain that it was in reality concrete and definite, but he can not prove his contention. Still, scarcely any one would wish to make such a contention. Vague, indistinct images are often like a child's drawing—they need interpretation. When we label them we know what they are, but to the uninstructed observer they may stand for a number of things. After calling attention to the existence of such ''general'' images, Watt then points out how illogical it would be

---

[23] *Op. cit.,* p. 364.

to infer from the existence of the general image the non-existence of the universal idea.

The second problem on which he touches under this heading· is the position of the mental image in our mental mechanism. The mere mention of the theory of types suffices to remind us that some authors write as if certain people made use of visual images in their mental operations to the exclusion of all others because they belong to what is termed the visual type. Watt points out that the kind of image used depends upon the ''task'' which the subject performs.[24] By changing the task the subject passes from the visual to the verbal type.

Another point that he makes is this: The mental image is not always a merely secondary phenomenon like the illustration in a novel. It may seem at times merely to accompany the word used as a stimulus. On other occasions it is clearly the starting point for the solution of the task. In all probability the mental image never comes into the field of consciousness without exerting some influence on the development of associations. Whether by inhibition or furtherance or direct suggestion of new ideas, it has its influence on the way in which the task is performed.

In conclusion Watt sketches the outline of his theory of thought. It is an attempt to account for the flow of consciousness. He first calls attention to the fact that consciousness is not discrete but continuous. He then asks what determines the entrance of an idea into consciousness? The chief factor is the ''task'' that the mind is attempting to accomplish. The tendency of one idea to reproduce another is determined in a merely mechanical way by the number of times that the two ideas were perceived together in the past. But the many possibilities, the many tendencies to reproduction, are limited by the ''task.''

In the much discussed problem of the relation between image, word, and concept, Watt admits the existence of all three and

---

[24] *Op. cit.*, p. 367.

does not attempt to explain away the concept in terms of imagery or words. From the statements of his subjects it was clear that there was a distinction between the word and the understanding of the word. One could exist without the other, therefore they must be distinct. But is the understanding of the word the crowding into consciousness of a number of dark associations? One hears nothing of such associations in the understanding of the word used as a stimulus; though in seeking for the word of response such associations do occur. The burden of evidence in his experiments rather favors the view that the understanding of a word is something other than crowding in of obscure associations. But for the final determination of this point he deems that further experiment is necessary.

The following year August Messer[25] published the next study of the Würzburg School. Dr. Watt was one of his subjects.

The general purpose of the study was expressed by the author as an attempt to investigate the conscious processes that are found in simple acts of thought. The method of the experiment was based on that of Watt's work, which has just been mentioned. There were fourteen series of experiments, some of which were taken from the "tasks" invented by Watt.

1. In the first series the subject was shown a word, and his task was to speak out as quickly as possible the first word that came to his mind.

2. In the second series the task was more restricted; the word of response had to be a word representing a coördinate *object*—that is, one that belonged to one whole along with the object represented by the given word.

3. In the third, the subject was to mention a coördinate *concept*—that is, one belonging to the same genus as the given word.

4. The response was to be any adjective.

5. A characteristic of the idea designated by the given word —but not its genus.

---

6. Remember an object belonging under the concept of the given word and make a statement concerning it.

From the seventh to the eleventh experiment two words were shown one above the other. The upper was to be read first. The subject's tasks were:

7. Express the relation between the *ideas* designated by the given words.

8. Express the relation between the *objects* designated by the given words.

9. In the ninth series the two words were the names of celebrated men and the subject was to pass on their relative value, expressing a judgment which had real claim to objective validity.

10. In the tenth series the persons, things, or conditions represented by the given words were to be compared and a judgment expressed; but the judgment was to be one of merely subjective value and express what would be the subject's preference.

11. In the eleventh, a noun and an adjective were shown to the subjects. He was instructed to regard the two words either as a question or an assertion, and where possible to pass a judgment about them.

12. In this series the subject was shown sentences or groups of sentences and his task was to understand them and take up a position in regard to them. The groups of sentences represented logical premises and conclusions formally correct.

In the last two series of experiments the subject was shown real objects or pictures.

13. He was to speak the first word that came into his mind.

14. He was to make a statement about the object or picture.

In the first series, though no special task was given, the subject made one for himself. He involuntarily sought a word that bore some relation to the given word. In other series also the tendency was noticed to specialize still further the task assigned.

In the visual imagery of the subjects there is again found

the "general image" mentioned by Watt. This proves to be an image so imperfect that the subject can designate it only by some such word as an animal, a bird, etc. Such an image may be spoken of as general because it can stand in consciousness for an entire class.

The author also gives some account of the motor imagery that his subjects experienced during the experiments. Then after a discussion of the process of association he passes on to a problem more closely allied to our own, the understanding of the word—the concept as distinct from word and imagery.

Generally the meaning seems to come with reading the word. But even in such cases the meaning is not a constant factor. It may exist in all degrees of perfection. The word may be scarcely understood at all. It may be perceived, but merely as a sound without meaning. Or the understanding may come partially with reading and take some time to grow. This latter form leads up to the case in which there is an actual separation between the perception of the word and the apprehension of its meaning. The conditions for the separation of the word from the apprehension of its meaning are as follows:

1. The strangeness of the word.
2. Incorrect reading of the word.
3. Equivocal character of the word.
4. Imperfect knowledge of the language.
5. Number and length of the words.
6. The occurrence of a purely automatic reaction on the basis of verbal association, *e.g.*, *Laut–Schall, Haustier–Maus.*
7.. Fatigue.
8. Excitement.

The "meaning" of the word was often something that the subjects found it difficult to explain. It was frequently expressed by such an expression as "I knew what was meant." The subjects were sometimes enabled to analyze this abstract "meaning" a little further. "The understanding of the word existed in the consciousness of that general sphere to which the word belonged" (p. 77). One of the subjects expressed it as "the consciousness that something appropriate could be associated." Sometimes the "sphere"-consciousness is identified with the generic idea to which the object belongs; again, with the entire domain in which an object belongs. For example, Subject 2 with the word of stimulus, "Hegel," said: "It seemed to me at first as if the word were 'Hagel.' As soon as the auditory image of '*e*' sprang into consciousness, there came a direction toward the History of Philosophy."[26]

At times the "sphere" of consciousness was an emotional element or word, or something similar. Again in the process of understanding, there was a consciousness of synonymous words or related objects, or some prominent characteristic of the thing represented by the word of stimulus. Sometimes the word instead of being understood in a general sense was taken in a special one, as where the word "garden" aroused the idea of a garden around a former home of the subject's family (p. 82). From all this it seems to the author extremely probable that in the process of understanding a word we have to do with phenomena of association and reproduction.

What part, if any, has the subject's imagery in his understanding of a word? The more perfect the imagery the less does it seem to cover what is meant by the general significance of the word. But the more schematic and faded the imagery, the less does it differ from the "meaning."[27] More important than the relation between the clarity of the image and the meaning, is the question: To what extent is imagery necessary to the signification? And here he says there is not one single example from which it is clearly evident that the understanding of the word was dependent on the awakening of a visual image. The most that can be said is that in a few solitary instances it was recorded that with the help of a visual image the meaning became clearer or more precise. But in the further progress

---

[26] Page 79.

[27] From what follows it is evident that the author does not mean to suggest that the meaning is nothing but faded imagery. The imagery fades into nothing, long before it gets anywhere near the "meaning," which may at times be clear without imagery.

of the experiment the subject's imagery plays an important part in the solution of the task. As to the understanding of the word of response, it often takes place before the subject can express his meaning, and when the word is found it does not always express fully the subject's mind. Sometimes too, the word of response is uttered before its meaning is understood.

The further sections of this work on the psychology of judgment, etc., are more remotely connected with our problem. The more kindred section on "Begrifflichen und gegenständlichen Denken" confirms still further the distinctions between word, image and concept.[28]

In immediate connection with the work of Watt and Messer is that of Dr. Schultze.[29] The foundation for his analysis is daily observation confirmed by his own experiments and those of others. His own experiments at the time of this article were to appear shortly under the title of "Beitrag zur Psychologie des Zeitbewusstseins."[30] He was subject in Messer's experiments and among his own subjects he numbered Külpe, Watt, and Messer.

His own work claims to be in the domain of descriptive psychology. His first problem, and the one with which we are concerned, is this: In the classification of mental processes is it justifiable to make a distinction between the sensible appearances of things and thoughts (*Erscheinungen und Gedanken*)? Originally he answered this question in the negative, but he was forced to give up this position on approaching the problem from the experimental point of view. The relinquishment of the old position seems to have required some effort, for he

---

[28] For a criticism of the technique in Messer's experiments, cf. E. Meumann, "Ueber Associationsexperimente mit Beeinflussung der Reproduktionszeit." *Archiv für die ges. Psychol.*, 9, 1907, pp. 117-150. Messer replied in his article, "Bemerkungen zu meinen Experimentell-psychologischen Untersuchungen über das Denken." *Archiv für die ges. Psychol.*, 10, 1907, pp. 409-428.

[29] F. E. O. Schultze, "Einige Hauptgesichtspunkte der Beschreibung in der Elementar-psychologie. I. Erscheinungen und Gedanken." *Archiv für die ges. Psychol.*, 8, 1906, pp. 241-338.

[30] Cf. *Archiv für die ges. Psychol.*, 13, 1908, pp. 275-351. See especially Sec. 11, pp. 329-333.

writes: "It cost me a great resolution to say, that on the basis of immediate experiment, appearances and sensible apprehensions (*Erscheinungen und Anschaulichkeiten*) are not the only things that can be experienced. But finally I had to resign myself to my fate" (p. 277).

His reason for doing so was that the data of appearances did not exhaust the content of experience. There are marked differences between appearances and thoughts. Appearances are apprehensible by the senses (*anschaulich*) but not so thoughts. Appearances are more or less localized. When there comes a pause in any series of appearances, during that pause we are conscious indeed of various sensations from the organs of the body—but is the consciousness of the pause the perception of such sensations? When there comes a blank over the mind, what is it that is lacking—sensation or thought? Thought. Thoughts are as much a matter of immediate experience as our sensations. Thoughts are not to be explained in terms of imagery. Thought can be perfectly clear and certain but the accompanying imagery is of various degrees of clarity or is altogether lacking. Thoughts are not feelings. (1) Because we can pass judgment upon matters of feeling without actually experiencing the slightest tremor of an emotional state. (2) We can experience feelings without any intellectual state connected with them, as for example, in certain unwarranted and inexplicable emotional states. (3) There is the same independence between the clearness and importance of thought and feeling in our mental states as there is between thoughts and images.

What then is our act of thought? Not the sensations that were active in the process of its acquisition. For we make frequent use of abstract concepts but seldom in connection with these concepts do we use the definitions and sensations necessary to their original formation. No sensation can conceivably exhaust all the characteristics of the concept. Concepts then are not sensations, not mental images, not feelings. They stand apart by themselves as special factors of our mental life.

The work of Watt, Messer, and Schultze was continued by Karl Bühler.[31] He thought it advisable to study the process of thought with materials which offered far more difficulty than the comparatively simple tasks of Watt and Messer. Accordingly such questions as the following were proposed to his subjects:

"When Eucken speaks of a world-historical apperception do you know what he meant thereby?" The subject had to answer with a simple yes or no, and then give an account of all the mental processes he experienced in arriving at his answer.

In a section on the Elements of our Mental Life of Thought he propounded the question—what are these elements, and which among them is the real bearer of the process of thinking? From the protocol of his subjects there is one group of mental processes that may be easily characterized—the sense imagery, whether visual, or auditory, or sensomotor. To this may be added the consciousness of space. There are also feelings and such states as doubt, astonishment, etc. But this is not all. The most important phenomena do not fall in any of the above categories. There is something else that possesses neither the qualitative nor quantitative characteristics of the senses. These elements of our mental life are what the subject characterized as "the consciousness that," etc., or more properly and frequently as his 'concepts' (*Gedanken*).

Do we think by means of imagery or by concepts?

The answer, based upon the subjective analyses given by his subjects, is that "what enters into consciousness so fragmentarily, so sporadically, so very accidentally as our mental images can not be looked upon as the well-knitted, continuous content of our thinking" (p. 317). Concepts then, not images, are the essential elements of our thinking.

What then is the concept? Not an image nor a series of images, nor the relation to a series of images. The concept is a unit, a mental element, the ultimate result of the analysis

---

[31] "Tatsachen und Probleme zu einer Psychologie der Denkvorgänge." *Archiv für die ges. Psychol.*, 9, 1907, pp. 297-365; 12, 1908, pp. 1-92.

of thought. As seeing is related to a sensation of sight as "sensing" to our sensations, so is knowing related to our thoughts. "Knowing" is distinct from "sensing." It may be accompanied by sensations but cannot be supplanted by them. Word imagery does not give us the signification of words. "A meaning can never be imaged but only known (Eine Bedeutung kann man überhaupt nicht vorstellen, sondern nur wissen)."

The solution of the task is not accomplished by a single series of concepts. Between concepts there goes on a great deal of thinking—the consciousness of the task to be performed—the relation of the given concepts to others and to the task. · The general consciousness of the task and the consciousness of manifold relationships constitute a kind of setting or background in which special concepts appear.

The understanding of words and sentences "is nothing less than a conscious logical relation, which brings into consciousness the connection between the thought · to be understood and one already known" (12, p. 13). In many cases understanding took place by the entrance into consciousness of a more general concept, and thereupon the subject knew how and why the idea before him belonged under that concept. The mere entrance into consciousness of the more general concept does not seem to suffice, but it must be perceived as bearing a relationship to the problem before the subject. Sometimes the thought that the given idea suggests is not a more general one, but one which the subject perceives to be identical with the given thought. Sometimes the given sentence is understood by its suggesting a thought that would prove it.

The analogy, between the process of understanding a sentence and the process of perceiving a geometrical figure, will be seen at once by comparing the above analysis of Bühler's work with our own section on the process of perception.[32]

The division of Bühler's work entitled "Ueber Gedankener-rinerungen" is of great interest and value in the study of memory, but bears less directly on the general problem before

---

[32] Below, pp. 127-139.

us. It tends to establish more and more conclusively the existence of an imageless process of thought—not, of course, directly and *ex professo;* but still, as Bühler's study unfolds, the possibility of accounting for thought by imagery decreases.

Shortly after the first section of Bühler's "Tatsachen und Probleme" had appeared, Wundt published[33] a criticism of the methods of the Würzburg School.[34]   He summed up (p. 358) the chief points of his criticism as follows:

(1) "The 'question experiments' are not experiments but self-observations under disadvantages.   Not one of the requisite conditions for psychological experiments is found in them—but they rather exemplify the very opposite of these conditions.

(2) "Among the old forms of self-observation they represent the most imperfect; they occupy the attention of the observer with an unexpected, more or less difficult intellectual problem and demand of him that over and above this he should observe the behavior of his own consciousness.

(3) "In both forms of its use the method of questioning is objectionable: As a question before the experiment it places self-observation under the very unfavorable condition of the pressure of examination; as a question after the experiment it opens door and gate to the disturbing influence of suggestion. In both forms it is most seriously prejudicial to self-observation by the very fact that the subject who must observe his own self is himself the object of inspection.

(4) "The representatives of the 'method of questioning' place themselves above the time-honored rule that in order to solve complex problems one must first be familiar with the simple ones that the former suppose.   As a consequence they confound attention with consciousness and fall into the popular error of believing that everything which transpires in consciousness can be followed out without more ado in self-observation.   The latter

---

[33] "Ueber Ausfrageexperimente und über die Methoden zur Psychologie des Denkens." *Psychologische Studien,* 3, 1907, pp. 301-360.

[34] For Bühler's answer see *Archiv für die ges. Psychol.,* 12, 1908, pp. 93-123.   Wundt replied to Bühler in this same *Archiv,* 11, 1908, pp. 444-459.

ground alone would sufficiently explain the bootlessness of the question experiments.''

If then the question experiments have not proved that thoughts are not images, but have proved nothing, how then are we to go on about the study of our processes of thought? Wundt outlines the method as follows:

(1) Self-observation under favorable conditions of solitude will teach:

(*a*) That thought precedes the language by which it is expressed.

(*b*) That this thought is made up of (*a*)' feelings that are adequate to the character of the thought and also (*β*) single fragments of images and words which suddenly come into consciousness and as suddenly disappear. These images seem to have been inhibited by the unfavorable conditions of the question experiments.

(2) The confirmation of the results of self-observation is to be sought in the experiments on association which show the tremendous importance which feelings have in such processes. Wundt refers to the discussion of ''idea feelings'' in his *Physio-logische Psychologie,* in which it is maintained, and perhaps proved, that in the development of a complex idea feeling often precedes imagery. From such experiments one may conclude that very faint ideas can betray their presence by very clear feelings; and it would be far better to speak of an unconscious substrate of ideas or even refer the total idea to this sphere of the unconscious than to talk of ''thoughts'' and the revised Aristotelian concept of imageless ideas. But the experiments on the compass of consciousness point to a gradation from the clearly conscious to the dimly conscious, and finally to a distinct break between the conscious and the unconscious. Consequently the partial elements of an idea are not to be referred to the unconscious but to the subconscious. They are elements in one complex process which is bound together in a single conscious whole.

A ''thought'' therefore in the Wundtian sense is a complex

of images and the ''adequate'' feelings which are involved in
their conscious unity. These feelings are combinations of his six
fundamental feelings which come together to form ever higher
and higher complexes. In each complex there is a total feeling
peculiarly characteristic of the complex and qualitatively different from the elements that constitute it. The total feeling
of the idea is ultimately analyzable into the six fundamental
elements of feeling—and the final product of their combination
is adequate to the character of the thought.[35]

Somewhat later E. von Aster, of Munich,[36] undertook a
criticism of the line of study which culminated in the work of
Bühler. The chief point of his criticism is that Bühler's subjects, in giving an account of their so-called concepts, were not
describing actually present mental states, as a man who describes a visual scene, but they were making mere declarations
concerning something which they had indeed experienced, but
whose real nature remained to be explained. He himself leaves
the problem of the nature of our ''thoughts'' to future research.
His own opinion seems to be that our thoughts are in some
manner composed of sensations and mental images and are not
mental processes different from the currently recognized
elements of our mental life.

A little later there appeared a criticism by E. Dürr,[37] one
of Bühler's own subjects. He finally came to an opinion which
takes on very closely the form of von Aster's objection.[38]

The designation of a mental process as a thought is by no
means a description of the character of the thought. The main
issue between Dürr and Bühler is in the analysis of the

---

[35] This analysis is based not merely on the article in the *Psychologische
Studien*, but also on various portions of Wundt's *Grundzüge der physiologischen Psychologie*. For a criticism of Wundt's opinion see the last
chapter of the present monograph, pp. 184-187.

[36] ''Die psychologische Beobachtung und experimentelle Untersuchung
von Denkvorgängen.'' *Zeitschrift für Psychologie*, 49, 1908, pp. 56-107.

[37] ''Ueber die experimentelle Untersuchung der Denkvorgänge.'' *Zeitschrift für Psychologie*, 49, 1908, pp. 313-340.

[38] Bühler in his answer denied that Dürr's objection was the same as
von Aster's. Bühler, ''Zur Kritik der Denkexperimente.'' *Zeitschrift
für Psychologie*, 51, 1909, p. 118, note 1.

"thoughts" to which Bühler's experiments had given so much prominence. Dürr would be far from agreeing with von Aster that our thoughts are ultimately reducible to sensation and mental imagery. Dürr's point of view can best be expressed in his own words:

"Bühler expressly stated that thoughts are not mental images (*Vorstellungen*) and that they have nothing in common with sensations. Now, the next question that arises is this: In our representative mental processes is there not something besides sensation; and if so, what is the relation of our thoughts to this plus?"[39]

Dürr thinks that along with our sensations there is our consciousness of time and space, of identity and similarity, etc. These things are not sensations or reducible to sensations. They might all be classed under the expression "consciousness of relationship," and this it is that will prove to be the ultimate analysis of thought.

In February, 1907, there appeared in the *Psychologischen Studien* a long article, "Ueber abstrahierende Apperzeption," by Kuno Mittenzwei."[40] It was an attempt of the Leipzig School to enter the field in which the ground had already been broken by the men of Würzburg. Mittenzwei preludes his experimental work with an historical account of the problem of abstraction from the days of Socrates to modern times. Between this historical account and his own experimental work there is no very close connection.

There are two distinct parts of the experimental work. In the first set of experiments the subject was required to direct his attention to a single circular disk (in reality the opening in an iris diaphragm). The disk was exposed twice in each experiment and the subject was required to tell what difference

---

[39] Page 326. I have taken some liberty in translating this last sentence. But the terminology I have chosen will, I think, give a true representation of the author's mind to English readers. The original is as follows: "Nun liegt doch die Frage nahe: Gibt es im Vorstellungsleben nicht noch etwas ausser den Empfindungen und wenn ja, wie verhalten sich die Gedanken zu diesen plus."

[40] *Psychologische Studien*, 2, 1906-7, pp. 358-492.

there might be in the size, position, or brightness of the disk in the two exposures.

In the second set of experiments the subject was called upon to observe a group of six disks, any one of which might undergo the above mentioned changes.

One is struck with the glaring difference between the task of the subject in these experiments and that of one who in real life forms what is termed an abstract idea of a group of objects. Mittenzwei's subjects had to look for a difference and neglect identity, whereas in abstraction one usually neglects all differences and finds identity. Hence, after reading the long dissertation on abstract ideas and having the appetite whetted for an experimental treatment of an old metaphysical problem, one is sadly disappointed to find that the author seems to have missed his problem. Instead of the question of abstraction he is really dealing with the perception of differences. But in spite of this serious defect Mittenzwei's experiments are not without value. One interested in the theory of spatial perception would find a very suggestive line of experiment. The problem of apperception is also helped along, even though the apperception is not —strictly speaking—that of abstraction in the logical sense of the word.

In the first series of experiments Mittenzwei measured the threshold for the perception of change,—A. Of size: Enlargement, reduction. B. Of position: Right and left, up and down. C. Of brightness: Increase, decrease.

For each of these changes he obtained two values: (*a*) one in which the subject was forewarned what change would take place, and (*b*) one in which the subject was not warned what kind of change to expect. In all changes except that of enlargement the threshold obtained when the subject was forewarned was smaller than when he was not warned. In the "enlargement" series it made no difference in the threshold whether the subject was or was not forewarned.

In the second series of experiments any one of six disks might be changed in size, position, or brightness.

It is here that the author stumbles upon some stages of development in the perception of difference. He does not name these stages, but, as the body of this work will show,[41] some of the points to which he calls attention as general phenomena are the same as certain stages that our own experiments revealed in the process of perceiving identity.

Under the name of *"der veränderte Gesamteindruck"*[42] Mittenzwei speaks of a perception of change without any knowledge of just what particular in the object was varied. The best description of this phenomenon is given in the subject's remark, "Das Objekt ist verändert, aber ich kann nicht angeben wie."

The author asks himself the question, how can such an indeterminate judgment be caused by such a particular and determinate change? This he explains by pointing out that:

(a) The second impression is involuntarily assimilated to the first, and

(b) The actual concrete change is often forgotten. Good observers have remarked, "Ich habe die Veränderung eben gehabt, aber ich habe sie schon wieder vergessen."

Under the heading of *"Partiell bestimmte Verschiedenheitsurteile"* the author describes what are really stages in the perception of difference that are a little more developed than the general impressions of change. The subject was required to give information on two points: (*a*) What was the nature of the change? (*b*) Where was it located? The determination of the location of the change comes first in the order of perception. The evidence for this lies in the fact that the erroneous or indeterminate judgments about the place of change are rare, while they are much more frequent in regard to the kind of change.

It is interesting to note how psychologically similar are the processes of perceiving identity and diversity. This will be apparent at once by the comparison of Mittenzwei's results with those reported below.

---

41 Cf. below, Section III, 2, pp. 127-139, more especially p. 129 ff.
42 Page 459.

The opposite of Mittenzwei's problem was taken up by A. A. Grünbaum under the title: "Ueber die Abstraktion der Gleichheit."[43] Historically it is connected with the Würzburg monographs and also with the first experiments of our own work. Grünbaum became acquainted with the method of research adopted in the present piece of research during the winter semester of 1904-5, when he was one of my subjects at the University of Leipzig. He has modified and developed the method, and for some purposes improved it. Instead of a series of exposures, each lasting but a fraction of a second, he exposed simultaneously two groups of figures for a period of three seconds. The subject was instructed to look for identical figures in two groups, thrown by a stereopticon upon a screen 4.25 m. from the subject. He was not required to fixate any point, but to distribute his attention equally over the entire field. After finding the identical figures, the subject was then to take notice of the others. After the time of exposition (3 s.) was over the subject was called upon to draw all the figures remembered, but especially the identical figures common to the two groups. After drawing what could be remembered, the subject was again shown the groups just exposed and was called upon to indicate the figures he actually recognized. The seeking and reproduction of the identical figures was termed the primary task, the noting and recognition of the remaining figures, the secondary task.

In reporting his results the author starts with the preparation of the subject for the task set before him and follows on down to the final determination of equality. The preparation of the subject for his task consisted in the picturing of a kind of frame in which there often flitted in and out vague figures. Two of the five subjects paid attention to some kind of sensory aid in their preparation. Three looked rather to the end before them and thus performed their task better than those looking to the means.

---

[43] *Archiv für die ges. Psychol.*, 12, 1908, pp. 340-478.

The process by which the task was performed manifested eight more or less distinct forms.

1. The method of exclusion.

The subject looks at one figure and then seeks one like it in the other group—not finding it, he takes another figure, and so on till he discovers the figure that.is in both groups.

2. Successive comparison without accentuation.

The subject looks first at one group and then at the other until he recognizes one figure as having been seen before. Before recognition the common figure does not require any special prominence over the other figures.

3. Successive comparison with simple accentuation.

This method is the same as that of number two, only that before the determination of identity one figure suddenly becomes prominent—is accentuated in a characteristic way ʌwhich can only be fully understood by one who has taken actual part in the experiments.

4. Successive comparison with accentuation and a realization of the task of the experiment.

In′ the former method the prominence of one figure seemed altogether independent of any idea of its being the one common to each group. In this method there is indeed no conjecture that the prominent figure might be the common one, but the subject is spurred on by something which one cannot express, except by some such words as the ''point of view of the task before him.''

5. Successive comparison with accentuation and the conjecture of identity.

This form of procedure is but a step removed from the last. With the perception of the prominent figure is united the conjecture that this may be the common one.

6. Rapid succession with accentuation of both identical figures.

In this form one figure is noticed and suddenly the other springs into prominence, sometimes so suddenly that the subject can not say but that the two figures were noticed simultaneously.

7. Simultaneous perception of the two figures.

In this form both identical figures are noticed simultaneously, and as a rule, none other.

8. Intuitive perception.

In this form the subject perceives one figure and knows at once that it is one of the identical figures without having seen the others.

Some of these divisions represent different methods of procedure, others are probably stages in one and the same method. The author, however, does not bring out this distinction. The intuitive method would have appeared less mysterious had Dr. Grünbaum pushed the inquiry a little further and taken into consideration our subconscious or unanalyzed mental content.

The primary task of the subject is the perception of a figure common to the two groups. In the fulfillment of the primary task it is interesting to notice the way in which the subject falls short of perfection in his reproduction of the common figure.

1. Instead of the perfect and complete form he will often give one that is schematically correct.

2. The subject will often draw a part of the figure and will know that something is lacking, but will be unable to supply it.

3. The correct form will be changed, but still remain recognizable. The most interesting case of this kind is what Grünbaum has called "mirror-drawing." The figure is drawn as if from its reflection in a mirror.

The success with which the primary task is accomplished decreases with the increasing number of figures in the groups. But the rate of decrease is not constant. It reaches a maximum in going from four to five figures in a group, and then rapidly declines.

The secondary task consisted in the reproduction of all the figures that could be remembered after drawing the common figure. The greater the number of figures in each group, the greater the number recalled. The ratio of figures remembered to those exposed decreases as the number of figures exposed increases. The author compared the fulfillment of the secondary task in recognition by the method of successive perception, with and without accentuation of the figures. It appears that the accentuation of one figure during the process of perceiving identity lessens the number of figures that are remembered over and above the common element. From this it would seem that with the accentuation of one figure the negative process of abstraction from the surrounding figures is already begun.

In connection with this conclusion is the evidence that the secondary task is fulfilled better when the primary task is not accomplished—or, in other words, the perception of the common element tends to obliterate the surrounding figures.

From the experiments of Grünbaum it would seem that the process of abstraction is brought about by an apperceptive accentuation and separation of the common element. On the other hand, the surrounding figures are forced into the background and lose something of their conscious value.

Here it may be well to append the abstract of the early experiments of this study which appeared in the report of the Fifth International Congress of Psychology, held at Rome in 1905.

THE PROCESS OF RECOGNITION.

"The problem of research undertaken in this set of experiments may be briefly stated as follows:

When a series of groups of figures (*e.g.*, a square, triangle, etc.) is represented to a subject and in each group one figure is always repeated, what mental process will be involved in recognizing that a figure has recurred in the series? It was not required of a subject that he should be certain that a figure recurred in each group, but only that he could say with certainty that some figure had been repeated.

Hitherto the problem of recognition has been mainly confined to the comparison of the sensations or perceptions of distance, etc., which the subject was to judge of as the same or different. But to surround the elements to be recognized with varying sensations brings the problem of recognition nearer to the conditions of real life and also enables us to approach by experimental methods somewhat closer to philosophical problems with which metaphysics has long been engaged.

In order to simplify the mental processes involved as much as possible the time of exposing a group of figures and the interval between exposures were both limited to a fourth of a second. A longer interval in either case would have given time for reflection, comparison, acts of the will to remember certain figures, and other rather complicated mental processes. The shorter interval eliminated in great measure these processes, for before there was time for reflection or comparison a new group of figures was represented.

The mechanism by which the expositions were given consisted of a metronome and Dr. Wirth's memory apparatus.

When a subject had perceived that a figure had been repeated, he was asked to give an account of the development of this process of recognition which he had just experienced. The subjective analysis thus obtained was in later experiments tested by limiting the number of expositions, so that the series of exposures ended before the observer had arrived at complete certainty. He was then asked to give an opinion and describe his state of mind. A control over the experiments was always kept by introducing from time to time a series of exposures in which no figure was repeated.

The following steps (naturally with various graduations) in the process of recognition were noted by means of this method:

1. An intimation of some kind of a figure being repeated without any knowledge of its form.

2. An intimation of some kind of a figure being repeated and a very imperfect idea of its form (*e.g.*, a dark spot, a cloudy spot which afterwards cleared up, an unsymmetrical figure, etc.).

3. Certainty that a figure is repeated but a clear image of only a part of the figure.

4. Certainty that a figure is repeated and a clear image of the form.

These steps seem to be but points in the more common and fuller order of development.

The subjects often remarked, when they first saw the common figure, it had already a tone of familiarity.

It sometimes happens that the blind intimation of a figure being repeated increases to certainty without any image of the figure being formed. This was especially the case when two figures were alternately repeated in a series of exposures.

The perception of the figure repeated has a tendency to force the other figures out of consciousness. *E.g.*, Subject K, in experiments where no figure was recognized as repeated, could afterwards draw the following numbers of figures as remembered: 3, 2, 2, 4, 4, 2, 1, 3. When, however, he had perceived a common figure he could draw as remembered only 0, 0, 0, 1, 0, 0, 0, 1.

It would thus seem that under the simple conditions of the experiments the progress of recognition is by no means a simple act, and that the formation of a mental picture is not the only or the most important factor.''[44]

---

[44] *Atti del V. Congresso internazionale di Psicologia tenuto in Roma, dal 26 al 30 Aprile, 1905,* pp. 286-287.

II.

THE METHOD OF RESEARCH.

1. The Problem and the Experiments.

It is very seldom, if at all, possible to reproduce in the laboratory the exact conditions of real life. Most of our experiments can only approximate more or less closely the actual occurrences in the external world. This is not, however, an insurmountable difficulty for experimental psychology. We have not one mind for the laboratory and another for the world. The same mental processes that take place in the world are observed in the laboratory, but under different conditions. The change in conditions is in the direction of greater simplification. The mental process of the laboratory is, as it were, a purified product and its true properties can therefore be more easily determined. The process of abstraction as studied in our experiments is certainly not the same as that of ordinary life. But it involves those very elements which are essential to the extra-laboratory mental operation. For this reason the present work is truly a study of abstraction.

The first method of experiment that I conceived of would have reproduced in the laboratory, almost exactly, the process of abstraction as it often occurs in actual life. It would have consisted in presenting to the subject a series of sentences, each containing a common idea. The subject's task would be to find the common idea, and report the mental processes he experienced in doing so. This method, however, is hard to bring under experimental conditions. I then thought of exposing to a subject a series of drawings. Each drawing would represent a single object, *e.g.*, a series of net-veined or parallel-veined leaves. The subject's task would be to pick out the common characteristic. Dr. Thorndike, of Columbia University, recently told me that he had thought of the same experiment, and suggested exposing a series of bilaterally symmetrical figures. By a little ingenuity a sufficiently complete material could be worked up, and this method of experiment would afford the opportunity for a valuable piece of research.[1]

But neither of these methods of experiments is as simple as the one finally adopted, which, though farther away from the actual conditions of outside life, still involves the essential factors of the process of abstraction. It may be well to note here that, when in the future I speak of "the process of abstraction," I mean, of course, the process as it existed under the conditions of these experiments. The analysis which results from our experiments is applicable to the real process of actual life only in so far as it appears that factors are analyzed in the laboratory which do occur in the more complete processes outside the laboratory.

The method I finally decided upon may be described as follows:

Let a group of geometrical figures stand for a group of qualities. Such a group has not indeed the unity that we see in the qualities of any object. However, when one is allowed but a single glance for one-fourth of a second at such a group, it really approximates the desired unity much more closely than would be expected. Let us expose in succession to a subject a series of groups of figures. In each group let there be one common element that constantly recurs. Of all the other elements that go to make up the groups of the series, let no two be the same. Representing our geometrical figures by letters, the following will give some idea of what is meant. Let us for example take a series of five groups with three figures in each group. This would be represented by:

1. A B C. 2. D A F. 3. G H A. 4. A I J. 5. K A L.

There is one element common to each group, and this one element is the common quality that is to be abstracted. The

[1] I wish to express here my indebtedness to Dr. Thorndike. It was his discussion of a paper I read in his class of Educational Psychology at Columbia University which was, although only indirectly, the first stimulus to the present work.

letters of the alphabet might serve for such an experiment were it not that their number is altogether too small. Instead of letters I used a specially designed set of figures.

Fig. 1.—The originals used were each about 1⅓ times as large as in this reproduction (see Fig. 2, p. 122 for actual size). The numerals at the side and bottom are merely for convenience of reference in the text. In these references, the first numeral (in lighter face) indicates position along the axis of abscissas; the second numeral (in heavier face) indicates position along the axis of ordinates. Not all of the figures were actually used. On account of their very evident associations the following were excluded: (1, 2)-(2, 2)-(5, 2)-(6, 2)-(11, 2)-(14, 5).

The figures possess one great advantage. On account of their strangeness, the process of perceiving them goes through a longer course of development and thereby one is enabled to detect points which it would otherwise be impossible to notice, or at least could be obtained with difficulty and uncertainty.

The groups of figures in the actual experiments (see cuts on pages 122 and 123) contained five figures instead of three. This drew out to some length the process of isolating and perceiving the common elements, thereby allowing a better opportunity to observe the development of the mental processes involved.

2. THE APPARATUS.

For the experiments in Leipzig, Wirth's memory apparatus with rotating disk was used. At the University of California I used Ranschburg's memory apparatus. Each performs the same function and the same disks may be used in either apparatus. Each rotates a disk and exposes suddenly a small surface and as suddenly removes it from view. In this experiment a group of five figures was exposed for a quarter of a second and then a blank space for a quarter of a second and so on till the series of twenty-five exposures came to an end or as much of the series was used as necessary for the experiment. It was at Professor Wundt's suggestion that I used this short time of exposure and interval between exposures. It tends to reduce the experiment to simpler and therefore more constant conditions by cutting out to a large extent such variable factors as reflection on what was seen, comparison, and voluntary association.

To beat time I have used both the metronome and the time sense apparatus, but generally the former, which is sufficiently accurate for the purpose. Care was taken to keep both these pieces of apparatus out of the room in which the observer was seated.

3. INSTRUCTIONS TO THE SUBJECT.

The subject was instructed to look for the repetition of some figure and to turn a switch, which stopped the rotation of the disk, as soon as he was certain that he had seen some figure repeated. It was not required of him to see this figure in each group as it passed by, but merely to be sure that he had seen some figure twice. He was told not to wait until he knew all about the figure but only to make sure that one and the same figure had occurred more than once. He was required at the end of the experiment to describe his state of mind during the experiment, and especially to tell what it was that he first noticed.

4. CLASSIFICATION OF THE EXPERIMENTS.

It soon became apparent that the method offered exceptional advantages for a genetic study of the process of abstraction. In handling the results and attempting to reduce them to some kind of order, the complex nature of abstraction became evident. And at the same time its analysis was greatly facilitated. Our five figures were found to constitute something of a unit which underwent a real process of breaking up. This was evidenced by the fact that the elements of a group have a different mental value after the perception of a common element than before.[2] Before the common element is noticed, the figures of any group have a tendency to persevere in memory, which varies with the focality of their perception[3] and with their own inherent attractiveness.[4] After the common element has been perceived the tendency of the other figures to persevere in memory is greatly reduced. The group is no longer what it was before it was broken up. This breaking up of the group is one of the several processes which form the mental complex that we call abstraction. The breaking up of the group is intimately bound up with the perception of the common element. Perception then is another factor in abstraction. The figure perceived is remembered and recognized again upon its recurrence. We have then four points in our preliminary analysis of abstraction: (1) The breaking up of the group; (2) The process of perception; (3) The process of memory; (4) The process of recognition. Each one of these has been made the object of experiment and form the four main headings in our experimental data.

---

[2] See below, pp. 124-127.

[3] See below, pp. 158-159.

[4] See below, pp. 122-124.

These experiments were commenced in Wundt's laboratory at the University of Leipzig. They were afterwards continued at the University of California. My thanks are due Professor Wundt for his kindly and valuable suggestions as to the method of experiment and also to Dr. Felix Krueger for his constant interest and assistance while I was working at Leipzig. I wish also to express my indebtedness to Professor Stratton and Dr. Wrinch, with whose valuable coöperation the experiments were conducted at the University of California.

The subjects who took part in the experiments were Miss Ball (B), Dr. Bessmer (Be), Dr. Brown (Br), Herr Blosfeldt (Bl), Miss Deamer (D), Herr Grünbaum (G), Dr. Krueger (K), Dr. Moore (Mo), Miss Mower (Mw), Miss Ross (R), Professor Stratton (S), Professor Eustachius von Ugarte (U), Mr. Wabeke (W), Dr. Wrinch (Wr), and Herr Ziembinski (Z).

III.

EXPERIMENTAL RESULTS.

1. THE ANALYSIS OF THE GROUPS.

(a) Isolation of the Common Element.

In abstraction some element or characteristic is always picked out from a group and is recognized as identical with that which was found in another group. In our experiments this element was the repeated figure. We may ask what is it in any element that accelerates the process of its isolation and perception? The answer as one might expect is—whatever attracts attention to the element. This may be the pure accident of its focal

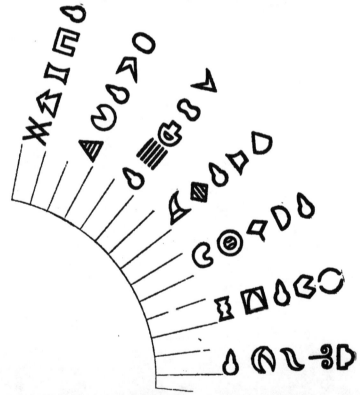

Fig. 2.—Showing grouping of 'elements' for actual display upon the disk, the common element following in the order 1, 3, 5, 3, 1, 3, 5.

perception. It may be the fact that it is rather larger than the other figures or blacker or more open.

Small but symmetrical figures, *e.g.*, 4, **12**, and 5, **12**, in Fig. 1, seem to pass by easily without being noticed. Another drawback is apparently the complication of the figure. This, however, is probably only apparent. The subject involuntarily waits to be informed about the complicated figures. Complication is, in itself, an advantage because it attracts attention. But the subject waits to know just what is repeated. In spite of instructions, he cannot stop the apparatus as soon as he is sure of the bare fact that a figure of some kind has been repeated.

The attempt was made to find out whether the sequence of position had any influence in the perception of the common element. If we number each of the five positions in a group

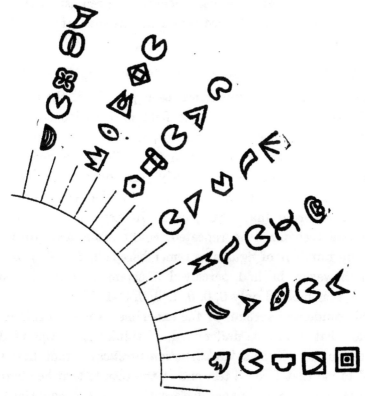

Fig. 3.—Showing the grouping of the figures when the sequence of the common element is altogether irregular.

of five elements 1, 2, 3, 4, 5, we have a means of recording this sequence of position. In the first group the common element may come in position one; in the second in two, and so on. We may have such an order as 1, 2, 3, 4, 5, 1, 2, 3, 4, 5 or 1, 3, 5, 3, 1, 3, 5 or 1, 5, 1, 5, etc., or the sequence of the common element may be altogether irregular. Whatever influence the sequence of position might have, it is so slight that it is obscured by the varying attractiveness of the figures themselves. So long as the common element does not come twice or oftener in the same position, the sequence of position seems to have but little effect. If it comes twice in the same position and the subject happens to see it, he involuntarily looks at the same place in the next exposition. In a word, then, it would seem that what was naturally to be expected is here the case. Everything that calls attention to the figure, either accidental circumstances or inherent qualities, tends to accelerate the process of its isolation and perception.

(b) The Disappearance of the Surrounding Elements.

Once the common element has been perceived, the surrounding elements are swept from the field of consciousness. They do not merely become less prominent, as one of the surrounding elements does when another is noted. They are forced into oblivion, usually complete. Rarely, one or two can still be remembered. In the passage quoted from the *Atti del V Congresso*[2] I reported that "Subject K, in experiments where no figure was recognized as repeated, could afterwards draw the following numbers of figures as remembered: 3, 2, 2, 4, 4, 2, 1, 3. When, however, he had perceived a common figure, he could draw as remembered only 0, 0, 0, 1, 0, 0, 0, 1."

This condensed account of the experiments needs explanation in order that it may be understood. I think that it was reading the account of Külpe's *"Abstractionsversuche"* that first suggested to me that I could test one of the results that he obtained in Würzburg. In his paper before the first German Congress

---

[2] See p. 115.

of Experimental Psychology he reported[3] that "negative abstraction has its most evident effect in the most difficult task" (p. 65). The greater, therefore, the absorption of the attention in the principal task, the less is remembered of the secondary task. It might therefore be concluded as a general law that the perception of the element to be abstracted has a tendency to obliterate the memory of the other elements. To test this result by our own method I asked the subjects at the end of the experiments to draw the figures which they remembered. Sometimes they had noticed a common element and sometimes it happened that they had seen no common element—either because there was none to see, or through some accident they failed to notice the common element that was present. Whether or not a common element is actually present made no very great difference so long as it was not noticed. I did not put this latter point to a careful test, and a common element that is not noticed at all may have some slight effect which is lacking when no common element is present. But there is a very great difference in the number of figures which can be remembered after an experiment in which no common element was perceived, and one in which the subject did see a common element. The numerals given above for subject K give the number of figures that he could draw in experiments where he had not seen, and again where he had seen, a common element. They seem to prove that the perception of a common element places the surrounding elements at a great disadvantage so far as their preservation from oblivion is concerned. But the figures as given are open to objection. It did not occur to me at the time that the series where no common element was perceived were generally longer than those where one was perceived. Hence there was a greater chance to remember more figures. However, the subjective analysis leaves no room for doubt on the matter. It is with great difficulty that one remembers the other figures after perceiving the common element. Whereas

---

[3] *Bericht über den I. Kongress für experimentelle Psychologie in Giessen, 1904,* pp. 62 ff.

when no common element is perceived, several figures are usually drawn readily and with ease.

However we are not left entirely to subjective analysis in the matter. Even when we take into consideration the relation of the length of the series to the number of figures remembered, we see that the memory of the surrounding elements is at a decided disadvantage whenever the common element is perceived.

The following results make this point clear:

SUBJECT K.

Common Element Not Seen.		*Common Element Seen.*	
Figures remembered.	No. of expositions.	Figures remembered.	No. of expositions.
		0	14
3	25	0	10
2	25	0	11
2	25	1	13
4	25	0	9
4	25	0	7
2	24	0	11
1	25	0	20
3	25	1	12
21	199	2	107

10.5 = Percentage of figures remembered when the common element was not seen.

1.9 = Percentage of figures remembered when the common element was seen.

SUBJECT W.

Common Element Not Seen.		*Common Element Seen.*	
Figures remembered.	No. of expositions.	Figures remembered.	No. of expositions.
		3	20
7	25	5	24
3	25	2	9
9	25	3	25
7	25	0	12
3	25	2	11
4	25	0	20
33	150	15	121

22.0 = Percentage of figures remembered when the common element was not seen.

13.2 = Percentage of figures remembered when the common element was seen.

SUBJECT G.

Common Element Not Seen.		Common Element Seen.	
Figures remembered.	No. of expositions.	Figures remembered.	No. of expositions.
		0	15
		4	21
2	25	0	4
4	25	0	4
5	25	0	4
0	25	1	7
5	25	0	8
3	25	0	7
6	25	0	4
3	25	1	13
28	200	6	87

14.0 = Percentage of figures remembered when the common element was not seen.

6.9 = Percentage of figures remembered when the common element was seen.

2. THE PROCESS OF PERCEPTION.

It would seem at first sight that the sense-perception of a given object is a matter which concerns, almost exclusively, the sensations involved in the act of perceiving. Suppose for instance that we have to do with the visual perception of some object. Then we can pick out the shades of brightness and the tints of color, and the spatial data given by the sensations arising from movements of the eye, and, if you will, the feelings of pleasure or dislike that may be involved. And this analysis having been completed, the task of the psychologist seems to have been done. The analysis is exhaustive and nothing more is required. This is a superficial view of the matter, but still a view which seems perfectly warranted until one seeks to find by experiment just what are the factors in the process of perception. It then appears that there are two factors. One may be termed objective. It involves the elements mentioned in the analysis just given. The other may be named subjective. This involves the correlation of the data of objective perception with that of past experience,—'apperception' in the Herbartian terminology; 'assimilation' in the Wundtian.

We may use the words 'perception' and 'apperception' for the objective and subjective factors in our apprehension of an object.

In the visual perception of an object there is one point which may be regarded as a stage of relative perfection, and that is the acquisition of a definite image. In the process of apperception there is no such stage which may be designated as perfect, nor indeed is it always easy to say whether or not the object has been apperceived at all.

For this reason we may take the acquisition of a definite image of an object as a kind of cardinal point and ask ourselves what stages of perception and apperception precede and what follow the clear visualization of the object. One of the first things which becomes apparent in going over the data of the experiments is this: Perception and apperception were intertwined in the process of apprehending the common element. Concerning the apprehension of the figures surrounding the common element the experiments give practically no data. It became possible to pick out stages in the apprehension of the common element because (a) the subject's attention was directed to seeing a figure repeat itself and thereby a special figure had to be looked for and impressed on the memory; and (b) the process of apprehension was often long drawn out, thereby giving an opportunity for the stages to be definite enough for detection.

The experiments in which the development of the knowledge of the figure was long drawn out were in the minority, and represent those cases where the process of apprehending the figure was relatively difficult. Or rather, they represent those cases where a focal perception of the common element was accidentally delayed. These are the hopeful cases for psychological analysis. Any one could look at two of our figures and tell at a glance whether they were the same or not. But in so doing he could not say with certainty just how he came to that conclusion, except that his eyes told him so. Perhaps here one really is concerned with a comparison of visual images. But even this is not clear. Suppose the rate of succeeding impressions is so rapid that there is no time to stop and compare images; suppose, too, that it is not possible to see the figure at will in the focal point of vision; what then will tell us that two succeeding figures are identical? This is really what was done in our experiments. The rapidity of the rhythm of exposition, the changing position of the common element, made focal perception at will an impossibility. As a result, the process of apprehending the common element often proceeded in stages that were well marked, and thereby it became possible to analyze it. For it turns out that the apprehension of a simple figure is not itself as simple as one might suppose. Certainly there is involved in it something more than mere seeing with one's eyes.

Some samples of the subjects' introspections are given below. These data were obtained by running through the experiments and picking out what the subjects described as the first thing to be noted in their apprehension of the common element. The samples given may be considered as answers of our subjects to the question, "What did you first notice?" if we exclude as irrelevant the remarks about certain figures which attracted their attention before any idea of a common element was present.

A. DATA ACQUIRED BEFORE A CLEAR PERCEPTION OF THE FORM.

1. *Feeling Tone:*
> An unpleasant unsymmetrical figure. (Bl.)

2. *Appropriate Mental Categories:*
> The idea of some kind of a figure; absolutely no determinate knowledge of just what kind; a very frequent case, and one that represents the earliest stage of perception.

> A horizontally lying curve.[4]

> Symmetry:
>> Subject noticed first that the figure was bi-laterally symmetrical, and only on seeing it somewhat later did he get an idea of the form. (Wr.) A pointed symmetrical figure. (Mw.) An unsymmetrical figure. (D.)

>> An idea of the figure changing its position, before an image of its form. (K.)

>> A common element similar to the one in the preceding experiment. (Mo.)

---

[4] A rare instance of spatial direction being given before a clear image. The figure was (8, 13). For an explanation of this manner of referring to the figures by number, see page 118.

Familiarity or Unfamiliarity:

Idea of a common element, then of something strange. (R.) In one series of experiments, figures were introduced which the subject had not seen before. Z said that with these disks he first noticed something new, and ·afterwards a special figure.

3. *Partial Perception of the Figure:*

Subject knew first that a common element was present, then that it was circular in form, then he obtained a complete idea of form. (G.)

A pointed figure. (Mo.)

An open kind of figure. (Mo.)

Subject knew that the figure was round, and had an idea of about how big it was, and could not get true form. (The figure was 10, 15.) (Mw.)

A narrowly oblong figure. (Mw.)

Something with top lines crossed. On stopping the apparatus knew exactly what the figure was. The image faded and the abstraction, something with top lines crossed, remained. (Mw.)

Subject first noticed something resembling a heart, then that it was different from a heart. (R.)

"I next noticed that the figure was pointed." (R.)

At end of experiment subject had forgotten whether the figure was a circle or a polygon. (R.)

A bar in the center with some kind of curves. This the subject attempted to draw, but failed utterly to produce the figure. (R.) Subject knows that the figure has a square in the middle, but cannot place the square where it belongs. (Bl.)

At end of experiment the subject was certain of two triangles with points together, and did not know just how the other lines were drawn. (Bl.)

At end of experiment subject remembered a diamond in the center of the figure, but was able gradually to build up the figure from this one fact and draw it (3, 3) correctly, (Bl.)

Had at first the idea of some kind of a polygon. (Bl.)

Thought a dark spot would turn out to be the common element, and so it did. (Bl.)

A narrow oblong figure. (D.)

Noticed at first a point and then a square. (D.)

First notices points and then something crossed; finally obtained the true image. (Gr.)

Knows that figure consists of two triangles, but does not know where to place the corners. (Z.)

At the end of the experiment the subject knew that the figure had something round in the middle. He was able to pick out the right figure (13, 11), on another disk, when it was placed before him. (Z.)

B. DATA ACQUIRED AFTER A CLEAR PERCEPTION OF THE FORM.

1. *The idea of a figure's orientation:*

In some figures a distinct axis may easily be picked out. They are built around this axis. And according to the position of the axis the figure may be turned to the left and right, or up and down, or it may be rotated around the central point of this axis. The actual position of the figure, as determined by the direction of the axis, is what I mean by the figure's orientation. It frequently happened that the subjects were in doubt about the orientation of the figure but felt perfectly certain about the form and did have, in fact, a correct knowledge of all the details of the figure. This leads one to suppose that since the orientation of the figure is not given with the perception of the shape and details of the figure's composition, it must require for its perception a distinct act over and above the act or acts of apprehension that are necessary to acquire a knowledge of the form.

Not only is the subject often left in doubt about the orientation of the figure, but he frequently is the victim of a delusion. It is an interesting fact that the subject would often be positively certain of an orientation that was just the opposite of the true one.

The explanation of this erroneous judgment is not certain. Grünbaum has termed the phenomenon mirror-drawing (*Spiegelzeichnung*), intimating that the figure is drawn as if from its reflection in a mirror. The errors, however, are not merely such as would be caused by drawing from a reflection in a mirror. They may indeed be right and left reversals, but they may also be up and down reversals or rotations of the figure, through an angle of ninety or of a hundred and eighty degrees; or errors which would be produced by combining the above alterations of position. As a possible explanation of the delusion, I would suggest the following: The figure was seen by glancing at it from another figure. This glance involved a movement of the eye. Ordinarily the orientation of a figure is judged at leisure, by moving the eye from one part of the figure to another. But in the rapidly disappearing figures, in our experiments, this was not always possible. The details of the form were seen first. This involved perhaps a single glance, which was an up and down movement of the eye, or a right and left movement or a rotation of the eyeball. This glance at the figure gave rise to the idea of its orientation. It was interpreted as a glance along the axis of the figure or from one point of the figure to another. There was no time to correct the first idea by a second movement of the eye. And the chance movement, in observing the figure, gave rise to the delusion of orientation.

From the fact that such delusions and doubts occur frequently, it seems clear that a true and certain perception of a figure's orientation requires a special mental act and is not ordinarily given with the perception of its form. Rarely, it may precede the full perception of the form.

The following stages of development give in brief outline an analysis of the process of perception:

The Stages of Perception.

1. The general idea of some kind of a figure being repeated. In this stage there is no definite information about the shape or nature of the figure whatsoever.

2. A more or less specialized idea of the figure. This idea of the figure may be expressed by perfectly general terms or it may be accompanied by a more or less perfect image.

3. A correct idea of the figure and clear knowledge of its shape, but doubt about or error as to its orientation.

4. A correct idea of the figure and its shape with a true knowledge of its orientation.

A pleasant or unpleasant tone of feeling may accompany any of these three last stages. I have never found it with the first.

From the above analysis the order of development seems evident. The subject does not pass from the individual to the general, from the concrete to the abstract, but just the reverse. What is offered to vision is individual and concrete enough. But what one first sees and holds on to is something that can fit into some kind of a mental category that the figure suggests. What one sees and does not hold on to, but at once forgets, takes no further part in the process of development. The mental category may be as wide as that conveyed by our idea of 'something.' Or again, it may pick out some special characteristic of the figure. There are, indeed, two classes of incomplete apprehensions of the figure used above and spoken of as appropriate mental categories and partial perceptions. The partial perceptions noted above must not all be put down as mere incomplete images. Once a subject said that she knew the figure was made of curved lines. She had not the slightest image of any curved lines nor any idea of how they were arranged. She attempted to draw some curved lines but failed utterly to reproduce the figure or any part thereof. Had there been a mental image of any part of the figure, that part could have been drawn. But there was no image. On perceiving the figure, it called up by association the idea of curved lines. That the figure belonged to the class of curved-line figures was apprehended clearly and remembered. The image of the curved lines was not remembered.

Another instance is that of Mw above. The final result was the memory of something with the top lines crossed. On stopping the apparatus she knew exactly what the figure was. The image faded and the abstraction ''something with top lines crossed'' remained.

Sometimes there may, indeed, be a piece of a mental image in the mind. But frequently, perhaps generally, this is not the case. The partial memory of the figure means simply that the figure called up some such general concepts as points or angles or curves, etc. The subject remembers the fact that the sensation fitted the concept at the time of perception. The sensation may leave no image behind it, but the memory of the fact remains.

We may regard the process of perception as terminating in a mental state representative of the figure and reproduceable in memory. The case of G above may be taken as representative of a good course of development. The subject knew (*a*) that a common element (12, **13**)of some kind was present. (*b*) He then knew that it was circular in form. (*c*) And finally he obtained the true mental image or at least a mental state that enabled him to reproduce correctly the figure he had perceived.

When the subject knew that some kind of a common element was present, he was not, of course, seeing a general idea of something with his eyes. On the contrary, perfectly individual and concrete sensations were being perceived. The process of perception was one of normal sensation, but in all probability not of focal vision. The process of apperception was the recognition of these sensations as belonging to the general concept "some kind of a figure." Later on, this concept was specialized to that of "a figure circular in form." Still later in the process of development, a mental picture was obtained representing the figure in its details.

However, *the mental image forms no essential part in the apprehension of a figure.* It is like the illustration in a book[5] which is useful but not necessary for the sequence of thought. The contention that the mental image forms no essential part in the apprehension of a figure is proved by the following experimental facts:

(*a*) Subjects Be, Bl, G, K, *M*, W, Z were at times conscious of a figure repeating itself before they could say anything more than that some figure was being repeated.

A figure was apprehended as repeating itself. Certainly, therefore, a figure was apprehended. But there was no image, nor any further knowledge of it than that it was some kind of a figure. Therefore the image is not necessary in the apprehension of the figure. One must not confound the visual image with the visual sensation. Without the sensations one might just as well have his eyes shut. There would be no apprehension at all, because nothing to apprehend. But in the resultant from the visual sensations, the mental image has no essential

---

[5] In the above statement I do not mean to call in question the conclusion of Watt about the utility of the mental image in forming associations. Mental imagery is very convenient and useful, but it is not the only element in the flow of thought, nor is it an essential element. Cf. Watt, *Archiv. f. d. ges. Psychol.*, 4, pp. 361 ff.

part because it may be lacking altogether. The residuum may be the bare fact of memory that the sensations did call up certain generalizations and did represent something belonging in their category.

(*b*) These results were not only obtained by a subjective analysis of the course of development after it had transpired; but were also confirmed by an objective test. Shortened series of expositions were given so as to cut short the process of development before it had arrived at completion. For example: Subjects who require on an average fifteen expositions to be sure that a figure was repeated, were given six or seven. They were asked at the end of the abridged series to describe their state of mind. In this way a kind of cross-section of the process of perception in its course of development was obtained, and a confirmation of the results of memory and introspection was secured.[6]

(*c*) The following series of experiments with subject Z is noteworthy in this regard. A series of disks was prepared in which there were two common elements. Common element *a* appeared in groups 1, 3, 5, etc. Common element *b* appeared in groups 2, 4, 6, etc. The two common elements were thus exposed to view alternately. The subject was told to stop the apparatus as soon as he was certain of one common element. He did not know whether or not there would be one common element in each group, or two in alternate groups, or none at all.

Experiment 1. Common Element (9, 12)–(10, 16).

    Result: The subject had a feeling that some kind of a common element was present during a period in which no determinate figure had as yet been noted. After four exposures he was sure of 9, 12 and when the apparatus stopped he saw 10, 16 by accident and knew that it had been there before. The subject then drew both figures correctly.

Experiment 2. Common Element (10, 15)–(10, 14).

    After ten exposures the subject drew 10, 15 and said that he had a feeling that another common element was present.

―――――――

[6] For a fuller account, see below, p. 163.

Experiment 9. Common Element (5, 12)–(4, 12).

The subject stopped the apparatus after nineteen exposures and said
that he was perfectly certain of some common element and that
there should be two, because two certainties kept crossing each
other in consciousness, but with no image. The feeling of certainty could not attach itself to any common element because before
it could do so, another feeling came of another common element.
He was unable to draw or tell anything about either of the common
elements.

Experiment 12. Common Element (14, 14)–(13, 14).

After nine exposures the subject stopped the apparatus and said that
he was certain of two common elements, but what they were he did
not know. He had a feeling that there was some common element,
but he could not find it. He judged that there were two because
of the difference in feeling between these experiments and those in
which there was but one common element in each group.

The remaining experiments of this series confirm these
results.

Further experiments were made with this subject, in which
disks were introduced having one common element in groups
1, 3, 5, etc. In groups 2, 4, 6, etc., there was no common element.
He sometimes mistook these disks for those of two common
elements, but he never said that there was a common element
on a disk where there was none at all. Nor did he mistake a
disk with one common element in each group for one with two
common elements.

These experiments make it perfectly clear that a common
element may be perceived and that, too, with certainty, while
in apprehending it there is not only no mental picture left in
the mind, but not even a more or less specialized general concept
of its form.

From the experiments of the above sections (*a, b,* and *c,* pp.
134 ff.), the conclusion is warranted that *a mental picture forms
no essential part of our apprehension of a figure.*

Taking perception as a general term to cover all the processes by which we arrive at a knowledge of the figure, we may
distinguish therein the following factors:

A. THE PROCESS:

   (a) *An objective Factor:*
      The sensations to which the figure gives rise. The reception of
      these sensations by the mind institutes a process of apper-
      ception.

   (b) *The Feelings:*
      Here feeling is taken in its strict sense, as pleasurable or dis-
      agreeable, or a feeling of tension, etc.

   (c) *A subjective Factor:*
      The sensations are recognized as representing an object which
      belongs to one or more mental categories.

B. THE RESIDUUM:

   (a) The memory of the fact that the object belongs to such or such
      categories.

   (b) The mental image.

   (c) The memory of the figure's orientation.

In the residuum, (a) is essential, (b) is not essential. I
cannot have an image of a figure without at least knowing
implicitly that it belongs to my mental category of figures.
But the experiments have shown that (b) is not essential, for
one can apprehend a figure without forming any mental picture
thereof.

The above view of the process of abstraction is borne out
in some important details by the work of Arthur E. Davies of
the Ohio State University.[7] This experiment regards two facts
as established.

"The first is, that perception is a mental process, not an act;
and the second, that the perceptual content undergoes a growth
before it can be definitely defined" (p. 189).

Our own experiments have made these points abundantly
clear. He also agrees with us in a conclusion that he puts forward tentatively. "Primitive psychic material does not seem
to be so much received from without, as developed from within."[8]
Taking this to mean in our own terminology that in the process
of perception there is both an objective and a subjective factor,

---

[7] A. E. Davies, "An Analysis of Psychic Process." *Psychological Review*, 12, 1905, pp. 166-206.

[8] *Op. cit.*, p. 200.

it must be put among the established facts of psychology; and indeed the subjective factor does have very much to do with the final product—perhaps more than the objective. The author points out three stages in the perception of the form :[9] (*a*) the perception of light. (*b*) An imperfect perception of the form. (*c*) A perfect perception of the form. That the perception of light should enter here as a stage prior to any perception of the form is indeed remarkable. The explanation, however, is to be found in the conditions of the experiment. The subject sat in the dark and the figures were illumined by a flash of light. Before any perception of the form could take place, there had to be a process of adaptation during which only light could be perceived. It is strange that the author makes no reference to adaptation as accounting for the perception of light prior to that of form. The flash of light, too, accounts for the feelings of tension, surprise, etc., to which so much attention was given by the author. However, it would be natural to suppose that a feeling of tension or excitement, or both combined in a weak emotion of surprise, might well precede the entrance of any objective perception into the field of consciousness.

The author notes that positive examples of association[10] were rare. The experience in our own experiment was that with some subjects they are plentiful enough, but rare with others.

In the following section, he seems to differ from us radically. "If therefore by association is meant the subsumption of a particular perception under a general idea or class, we do not find that such a procedure is characteristic of elementary psychic process."[11]

We take it, however, that his data on this point is negative. He did not find it to be so. And indeed he does not say that it is not the case. So, even here there is no real contradiction of results. The method used was not calculated to bring out that stage of perception which we found, in which there was no

---

[9] Page 176.

[10] We suppose that there is here meant association of the figures perceived with various ideas or objects of real life.

[11] Page 191.

image but only the bare knowledge of some kind of a figure. Davies exposed a figure by a momentary flash of light in a dark room. The subject was then required to give an account of his experience. There was always but a single exposure and no chance for a long-drawn-out development of the process of perception such as occurred in our own experiments. The op-opportunity for a longer process of development enabled the analysis based upon our own experiments to be more complete.

3. The Factor of Memory in the Process of Abstraction.

After the common element has been separated from the elements that surround it and perceived, it must be held in memory. The memory of the isolated characteristic or group of qualities is an essential element in the process of abstraction. Consequently it would seem desirable to investigate this process of memory as it occurred in our experiments.

There are three factors which are readily seen to affect the process of memory:

(*a*) The method of memorizing—visual or motor, or whatever method may be used.

(*b*) The effect of perceiving new groups between the time of the figure's first perception and its final recognition as a figure that has occurred more than once.

(*c*) The focality of perception—the chance falling of the figure in the focal point of vision, or more or less outside of it.

Each one of these points can be easily made the subject of experimental investigation and the three following sections give the results obtained:

(a) The Method of Memorizing.

During the course of the experiments it occurred to me to ascertain how long it would take to memorize a group of five figures so that they could be accurately drawn. While acting as subject in these experiments I discovered that this was largely dependent upon the method of memorizing. At first sight it would seem that in looking at a group of figures and attempting to get them in mind for future reproduction, one has to do with a process of memorizing by visual imagery. But one has but to attempt the task to discover that besides the visual image there is something else which is a powerful aid to memory. And this is a more or less complete mental analysis of the figures, an analysis which it is utterly unnecessary for the subject to put in words. What are the figure's more elemental parts? How are they related? Does it resemble anything in real life? Such factors as these are elements which, most will admit, do not belong to the visual sensation, as such, nor to its more or less perfect replica, the visual image. The attempt to picture an object so as to be able to see it clearly with the mind's eye, and if need be, draw it, is one mental process. The effort to analyze an object, to see what it is made of, what it resembles, its possible use, etc., is another mental process. And while the two may go hand in hand, they need not; and it is possible to memorize by either method.

Experience, however, would indicate that visualization without analysis is rare and difficult. However, these are two very distinct methods of memorizing; and while it is not possible to use either in an absolutely pure and unadulterated form, still it is possible to make either visualization or analysis the predominating feature in the method of memorizing. This was attempted in the following series of experiments. The method of experiment was very simple. A group of five figures was exposed for a constant time and the subject was called upon to memorize the group by one or the other method. At the end of the time the group was covered and the subject called upon to draw what he remembered. The drawings were then rated, an approximately perfect drawing being given a credit of 1. An imperfect drawing, but still recognizable as being intended for one of the figures exposed, was given a credit of 0.5. An utterly unrecognizable drawing was given a credit of 0.1. An omission was counted as zero. It is not always possible to assign a drawing with certainty to one of the three gradings. However, it is generally fairly easy and is better than calling everything perfect or zero.

After a little experimenting it became evident that the method of analysis had a decided advantage over that of visualization. After this was noticed, there might be a subconscious tendency to favor the marking by analysis and thereby strengthen the evidence for the point maintained. But however much one might do this I am sure that no system of conscientious marking could turn the balance in favor of visualization. To offset any such tendency I was a little stricter in marking the results obtained in memory by analysis than those obtained by visualization. And I believe that the markings given for analysis are a trifle too low.

A much more serious difficulty is that which arises from the attempt to exclude all analysis of a figure when one is trying to get a visual image of it fixed in the mind. Associations crop up spontaneously, and one simply cannot exclude all analysis of the figure. The subjects were instructed that when they were attempting to memorize by visual imagery they were not to mind any involuntary associations or analyses of the figure that might spring up, but still not to make any great effort to suppress them. The result is that the two sets of experiments really represent memory by visualization without attempt at analysis or association, and memory by analysis and associations without any attempt to acquire a definite mental image. It is much easier to memorize by analysis to the exclusion of imagery than *vice versa*. Subjects often remarked that figures were remembered by some association rather than by imagery when they were attempting to memorize by visualization. But it seldom happened in attempting to memorize by analysis and association that the figure was recalled by its visual image suddenly appearing without any apparent associational connections. As a result of this the markings for memory by visualization are considerably higher than they would be if the method could have been used in absolute purity.

SUBJECT B.

Sept. 27, 1907.		Oct. 11, 1907.	Oct. 25,1907.
Imagery.	Association.	Imagery.	Association.
0.8	4.0	2.1	2.6
0.4	1.7	2.1	2.2
0.4	2.1	0.4	3.2
1.2	2.1	3.0	1.2
0.3	2.0	2.2	2.2
1.6	2.1	1.5	1.5
6) 4.7	6)14.0	3.0	1.7
		1.3	3.5
0.8	2.3	1.1	2.6
		2.0	
		1.2	9)20.7
		1.5	
			2.3
		12)21.4	
		1.8	

Oct. 4, 1908.		Oct. 31, 1907.	
Imagery.	Association.	Imagery.	Association.
2.5	3.0	1.5	3.1
2.0	3.2	0.1	2.1
2.1	2.1	3.1	3.2
2.1	3.0	1.6	2.2
1.1	1.5	1.5	3.0
2.0	3.5	5) 7.8	5)13.6
6)11.8	6)16.3	1.6	2.7
2.0	2.7		

SUBJECT R.

Sept. 26, 1907.

Imagery.	Association.
2.6	5.0
2.0	4.5
1.0	5.0
3.0	2.5
3.1	5.0
1.5	
—	5)22.0
6)13.2	—
—	4.4
2.2	

Oct. 3, 1907.

Imagery.	Association.
3.0	5.0
3.0	1.0
1.1	3.0
4.0	4.1
2.2	2.0
2.9	4.4
2.7	3.0
—	4.0
7)18.9	—
—	8)26.5
2.7	—
	3.3

Oct. 10, 1907.

Imagery.	Association.
2.2	2.7
4.5	3.6
3.0	5.0
2.5	2.7
2.0	4.5
5.0	4.0
3.0	3.5
3.1	4.1
1.5	5.0
1.3	5.0
2.1	3.1
2.5	5.0
—	—
12)32.7	12)48.2
—	—
2.7	4.0

SUBJECT Mo.

April 18, 1907.

Imagery.	Association.
2.0	4.0
2.0	5.0
2.0	4.0
2.0	4.0
2.0	4.0
—	—
5)10.0	5)21.0
—	—
2.0	4.2

April 25, 1907.

Imagery.	Association.
4.0	3.0
2.5	5.0
2.0	3.0
2.0	4.0
3.0	4.5
2.0	5.0
—	—
6)15.5	6)24.5
—	—
2.6	4.1

Oct. 8, 1907.		Nov. 7, 1907.	
Imagery.	Association.	Imagery.	Association.
2.0	4.5	3.0	4.0
2.0	5.0	2.0	4.0
1.0	4.0	3.0	5.0
4.0	3.0	3.0	3.0
3.0	4.0	2.0	4.0
4.0	5.0	3.0	3.0
3.0	4.0	3.0	3.0
3.0	5.0	2.0	5.0
2.0	4.0	3.0	4.0
3.0	4.0	3.0	4.0
10)27.0	10)42.5	10)27.0	10)39.0
2.7	4.2	2.7	3.9

The above tables show in every case a decided advantage in favor of memory by association and analysis, over memory by imagery. It would therefore seem as if the psychological factors in the analysis and association of a figure add greatly to the mind's power of retaining and reproducing it. An objection, however, was suggested by a friend who was not inclined to give up so readily the primary importance of mental imagery in the process of memory. Perhaps in memory by association, he held, there is brought into play the motor imagery which is inhibited by the attempt at visualization. So that in what is termed memory by association we have really memory by visual imagery plus motor imagery, and therefore this is naturally the more favored form. That such was not the case is evident not only from evidence to be given later, but from the record that was kept of the cue by which the subjects fixed the figures in mind in memorizing by association. Not once did they mention any feeling of movement, as of outlining or drawing the figure or its parts, but the associations were always such as connected the figure with some known object, or analyzed it into parts, or some kind of description was given which was of itself insufficient to express the subject's full concept of the figure, but stood as a symbol for his mental state in regard to it.

Below are a few random samples of such associations, divided into three classes:

(*a*) Associations which connect the figure with an object in real life.

(*b*) A description which indicates some kind of an analysis of the figure.

(*c*) A designation which really expresses the subject's inability to associate or analyze the figure in the given time, but which nevertheless serves as a symbol of the figure and aids in its recall.

A. OBJECT.	B. ANALYSIS.	C. SYMBOL.
Scroll of paper.	Circle.	Curlycue.
Melon.	Curved figure with dot.	
A kind of handle.	A kind of hexagon.	Funny figure.
Star.		Something upside down.
Tulip.	A kind of oblong.	
Heart.	A kind of square figure.	The well-known figure.
Swastika.	A half-circle.	The unassociated figure.
Diamond with handle.	A kind of scroll.	
Dumb-bell.	Curves.	
Two turnips.		
Necktie.	Dots.	
	Squares	
	Points.	
	Pentagon with dot.	
	Cut triangle.	
	Cut quadrangle.	
	Something long and narrow with points.	

On looking over this list of associations one might be inclined to say that this so-called memory by association and analysis is really nothing but a process of naming the figures and remembering the words used. That might be so if the catch-word used to designate the figure generally were sufficient to express it truly. But that is not the case. The figure is never completely described. And the subject's task is not to remember his description of the figure but to remember the figure so as to be able to draw it. The word or words used serve to fix and crystallize the mental state that was experienced in perceiving the figure. They are not that mental state nor do they fully express it. Why? Because there is more in that mental state than is given in the word. And how do we know this? Because the subject draws more than his words express.

It is an important thing to ascertain the real value of motor imagery in memorizing such figures as were used in our experiments. It is not evident from inspection that it is either inferior or superior to "memory by association." Accordingly a method was devised by which the value of motor imagery could be tested. The subject was allowed to trace the figures with a pointer in one set of experiments, thereby giving him an opportunity for the development of motor imagery. This set of experiments was compared in each sitting with a "visual" and "association" set. The time allowed for each experiment was that which sufficed for the subject to trace five figures, which varied from 10 to 13 seconds, with the three subjects. Each subject, however, had for visualization and association the time that allowed him to trace comfortably the five figures. The order in which the experiments are printed is that of the experiment.

SUBJECT BR.

Aug. 24, 1908.

Visual.	Motor.	Association.
1.0	3.0	4.0
1.5	3.5	3.5
0.5	3.0	3.5
3.1	2.6	3.5
2.6	1.1	3.1
1.1	2.6	3.6
6) 9.8	6)15.8	6)21.2
1.6	2.6	3.5

Sept. 28, 1908.

Association.	Visual.	Motor.
3.5	2.0	2.5
3.0	1.6	3.0
5.0	2.0	1.1
3.5	1.5	1.0
2.0	2.1	3.0
2.0	1.1	1.0
3.6	2.0	3.0
7)22.6	7)12.3	7)14.6
3.2	1.7	2.1

Oct. 5, 1908.

Motor.	Association.	Visual.
1.6	3.5	3.5
3.0	4.0	1.2
2.6	4.0	1.0
2.0	3.5	2.5
2.5	3.0	2.5
2.0	3.1	2.1
6)13.7	6)21.1	6)12.8
2.3	3.5	2.1

Oct. 19, 1908.

Visual.	Association.	Motor.
3.0	2.5	2.5
1.0	2.6	1.5
2.0	4.5	3.5
2.0	3.0	1.0
2.5	4.0	1.0
2.0	3.6	1.0
6)12.5	6)20.2	6)10.5
2.1	3.4	1.7

SUBJECT S.

Aug. 26, 1908.

Visual.	Motor.	Association.
2.0	4.0	5.0
4.0	1.5	4.0
1.0	2.1	5.0
2.1	2.0	4.0
1.0	2.5	4.0
2.5	1.5	1.0
6)12.6	6)13.6	6)23.0
2.1	2.3	3.8

Sept. 3, 1908.

Association.	Visual.	Motor.
4.0	2.0	3.0
3.5	3.0	4.0
4.5	1.0	1.5
4.5	4.0	1.5
3.5	4.0	2.0
5.0	1.5	3.0
2.6	4.0	2.5
7)27.6	7)19.5	7)17.5
3.9	2.8	2.5

Sept. 10, 1908.

Motor.	Association.	Visual.
4.1	2.1	3.1
2.0	4.0	2.0
4.0	4.0	1.0
2.0	3.0	1.5
1.0	4.0	3.0
3.0	4.0	2.0
1.0	3.1	3.1
7)17.1	7)24.2	7)15.7
2.4	3.5	2.2

Sept. 17, 1908.

Association.	Motor.	Visual.
4.0	3.5	2.0
2.0	6.0	3.0
4.0	1.6	3.5
5.0	2.0	2.0
5.0	3.0	2.0
5)20.0	5)16.1	5)12.5
4.0	3.2	2.5

Sept. 24, 1908.

Visual.	Motor.	Association.
3.0	2.5	4.0
2.5	3.5	1.5
3.0	3.0	3.1
3.0	2.5	4.0
1.0	1.0	3.5
1.0	2.0	2.5
1.6	3.5	3.5
2.5	2.5	4.0
8)17.6	8)20.5	8)26.1
2.2	2.6	3.3

SUBJECT WR.

Aug. 27, 1908.

Association.	Visual.	Motor.
5.0	4.0	5.0
4.5	2.5	3.5
2.5	3.0	3.1
4.0	3.0	1.5
3.5	4.0	3.5
4.5	2.5	3.5
3.5	2.5	1.0
7)27.5	7)21.5	7)21.1
3.9	3.1	3.0

Sept. 3, 1908.

Visual.	Motor.	Association.
2.0	4.0	4.0
4.0	1.0	5.0
4.0	3.0	4.5
2.5	2.0	5.0
2.0	2.0	4.0
5)14.5	5)12.0	5)22.5
2.9	2.4	4.5

Sept. 10, 1908.

Motor.	Association.	Visual.
4.5	2.5	4.1
4.5	4.5	3.0
4.0	5.0	3.0
4.0	4.1	4.1
2.5	4.0	1.0
5)19.5	5)20.1	5)15.2
3.9*	4.0	3.0

Sept. 17, 1908.

Association.	Motor.	Visual.
5.0	3.0	3.0
4.0	4.0	3.5
3.5	0.5	2.5
5.0	3.0	2.5
2.5	3.0	2.0
5)20.0	5)13.5	5)13.5
4.0	2.7	2.7

* In this set seven figures were recalled by involuntary association. Were these excluded the average would be reduced to 2.5.

Oct. 1, 1908.

Visual.	Association.	Motor.
4.0	4.5	4.0
2.5	5.0	4.0
3.0	5.0	2.5
2.5	4.0	4.0
1.5	4.0	3.0
5)13.5	5)22.5	5)17.5
2.7	4.5	3.5

SUBJECT BR.

Table of Averages.

Association.	Motor.	Visual.
3.5	2.6	1.6
3.2	2.1	1.7
3.5	2.3	2.1
3.4	1.7	2.1
4)13.6	4) 8.7	4) 7.5
3.4	2.2	1.9

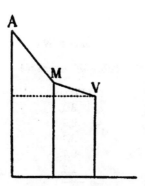

Figure 4, showing the relation between memory by association (A), motor (M), and visual (V) imagery for Subject Br.

SUBJECT S.

Table of Averages.

Association.	Motor.	Visual.
3.8	2.3	2.1
3.9	2.5	2.8
3.5	2.4	2.2
4.0	3.2	2.5
3.3	2.6	2.2
5)18.5	5)13.0	5)11.8
3.7	2.6	2.3

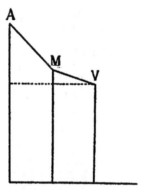

Figure 5, showing the relation between memory by association (A), motor (M), and visual (V) imagery for Subject S.

SUBJECT WR.

Table of Averages.

Association.	Visual.	Motor.
3.9	3.1	3.0
4.5	2.9	2.4
4.0	3.1	3.9
4.0	2.7	2.7
4.5	2.7	3.5
5)20.9	5)14.5	5)15.5
4.2	2.9	3.1

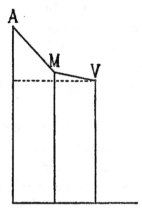

Figure 6, showing the relation between memory by association (A),
motor (M), and visual (V) imagery for Subject Wr.

These tables and figures show a decided advantage for
memory by association over memory by imagery. They show
besides that, so far as this advantage is concerned, it makes
no difference whether the imagery be visual or motor. In
motor-imagery we really have motor plus visual, for the subject
necessarily looks at the figures while tracing them. So that
even the combined effect of visual and motor imagery cannot
equal the results obtained by analyzing and associating the
figures.

(b) Memory as Related to the Sequence of the Surrounding Figures.

In the process of abstraction one group of sensations after
another is perceived by the mind. In each one of these groups
some common element is always contained. The moment arrives when this common element becomes separated from those
that surround it, and approaches the focal point of consciousness. This is, as we have seen, not an instantaneous act but a
process with more or less definite stages, and can under circumstances consume a relatively long time. In the meanwhile one
group of impressions after another falls upon the mind. What,
we may ask, is the effect of these impressions on the subject's
memory of the common element? One might jump to the

conclusion that they tend to obliterate the memory of the common element. Still, one cannot be sure of this, off-hand; experiments have surprises in store.

Angell and Harwood found that distractions between a normal and compared stimulus not only did not always decrease the accuracy of recognition, but that at times they even increased it.[12] A very different result obtains where it is not a question of recognizing a stimulus but reproducing that which has previously been learned. Under these conditions the effect of sensory stimuli between the time of memorizing and of reproduction is to obliterate that which the subject had learned. Bigham found[13] the following average errors under these conditions:

	Empty interval	Optical filling	Acoustical filling
2 sec.	25.2	29.4	34.7
10 sec.	28.8	31.0	36.0
30 sec.	31.1	33.0	37.1

We might rest upon the results of Bigham and conclude that when a number of new figures are noticed after the perception of the common element they will tend to obliterate the memory of the common element. The lapse of time between the first and the second perception of the common element is not the only factor which tends to obliterate the common element. Succeeding impressions have a positive tendency to impair the subject's memory for the common element which has attracted his attention. However it seemed best not to rest content with experiments made under conditions that were not precisely the same as those under which we studied the process of abstraction. We put the point to an actual test.

The method of experiment was as follows: The subject first saw three groups of figures. He was instructed to fixate a given position in these groups—*i.e.*, always the first, counting from

---

[12] Angell and Harwood, ''Discrimination of Clangs for Different Intervals of Time, Part I.'' *Amer. Journ. Psychol.*, 11, pp. 67-79; Part II, *ibid.*, 12, pp. 58-79.

[13] J. Bigham, ''Memory.'' *Psychol. Review*, 1, 1894, p. 459.

left to right, or the second, or the third, etc. After these three groups came a fourth exposure. In this there was but one figure, which might be in any one of the five positions. After this came a certain number of groups—five, or twenty-one, or twenty-one blank spaces—according to the nature of the experiment. At the end of each experiment the subject's task was to draw the isolated figure of the fourth exposure.

The reason for varying the distance between the point of fixation and that of the exposure of the figure was to reproduce that condition of the previous experiments in which the subject is still unsatisfied with his knowledge about the common element. I first compared the condition of memory after five exposures with that after twenty-one. The subjects were rated as in the previous experiments on memory, and then an average of all experiments was taken. For memory after five exposures the general average for the subjects (twenty-six experiments) was 0.46. For memory after twenty-one exposures the general average for three subjects (thirty-one experiments) was 0.34. We thus see that increasing the number of exposures, after the perception of a figure, has a tendency to decrease the accuracy of the memory. I then compared the condition of memory after twenty-one groups of figures had followed the isolated figure with the condition when twenty-one blank spaces followed the isolated figure. The average in the first instance for the subjects (twelve experiments) was 0.67. In the second instance the average for three subjects (fifteen experiments) was 0.77. The perception of new figures seems therefore to have a tendency to obliterate the memory of the one already perceived. The element of practice, however, has almost doubled the markings, so too much reliance cannot be placed on these preparatory experiments.

It seemed possible to get results more quickly if we had a material in which each element was more homogeneous. One figure is so much more attractive than another and has so many more possibilities of association that the element of chance enters in to obscure the results. Consequently a set of numbers was prepared. In each number there were three digits. In no number was the same digit repeated. A zero never occurred. An arithmetical sequence of the digits was avoided. Such numbers as the following were therefore excluded: 112, 120, 123. The order of experiments remained the same as before, only instead of figures we had numbers consisting of three digits each. A comparison was then made between the memory of an isolated number after twenty-one blank spaces had followed, with that after twenty-one groups of five numbers each had been exposed.

The memory was rated as either good or bad. If the subject recalled two or more digits correctly, his memory of the number was rated good; if he gave less than two digits correctly it was rated bad. The results are given below. The series with the vacant spaces are designated by V, the series with the twenty-one groups of figures are designated by ''21.'' Δ indicates the difference in position between the point of fixation and the occurrence of the isolated element. Under *M* is given the rating of the subject's memory—good (g) or bad (b).

SUBJECT D.

V			"21"	
Δ	*M*		Δ	*M*
1	g		1	b
0	g		1	g
1	g		0	b
1	g		1	b
0	g		0	g
1	g		1	b
	g			b
	g			b
1	g		1	b
2	b		2	b
2	g		2	b
2	g		2	g
0	g		0	b

| 12g — 1b | | | 3g — 10b | |

SUBJECT Mw.

V			"21"	
Δ	M		Δ	M
0	b		0	b
0	g		0	b
0	b		1	b
1	g		1	b
0	g		0	g
0	g		1	b
1	g		1	b
1	g		0	b
0	g			
	7g — 2b			1g — 7b

SUBJECT R.

V			"21"	
Δ	M		Δ	M
1	g		0	b
1	g		1	g
0	g		1	g
0	g		0	g
1	g		1	g
1	g		2	b
2	b		2	b
2	b		0	b
0	b		0	b
0	b		0	g
0	g			
	7g — 4b			5g — 5b

For all three subjects we have in the V Series 26g-7b and in the "21" Series 9g-22b. It is evident by inspection that memory is better in the V series. We may, however, express this better by using one of *P*earson's auxiliary methods of correlation.[14] The one best adapted to the data at hand is

$$r = \sin \frac{\pi}{2} \frac{\sqrt{ad} - \sqrt{bc}}{\sqrt{ad} + \sqrt{bc}}$$

[14] Cf. Spearman, ''The Proof and Measurement of Association between Two Things.'' *Amer. Journ. Psychol.*, 15, 1904, p. 82.

In this case a is the number of times the V series was good; b is the number of times it was bad; c is the number of times the "21" series was good; d the number of times it was bad. Accordingly we have

a	b	c	d
Vg	Vb	"21" g	"21" b
12	1	3	10
7	2	1	7
7	4	5	5
26	7	9	22

$$r = \sin \frac{\pi}{2} \; \frac{\sqrt{(26).(22)} - \sqrt{(7).(9)}}{\sqrt{(26).(22)} + \sqrt{(7).(9)}} = 0.71$$

$$\text{Probable error} = \frac{1.1}{\sqrt{n}} = \frac{1.1}{\sqrt{33}} = \pm .19$$

$$r = 0.71 \pm .19$$

(c) Memory as Related to the Focality of Perception.

To give some idea of the decrease in the accuracy of the memory with the distance of the object from the point of fixation, I plotted a curve from the few preparatory experiments of the previous section. It happens to be of a smoothness that is not warranted by the few experiments and which I believe is somewhat accidental. In spite, however, of some objections that can be made to it, its main points represent fairly the decrease in the accuracy of the reproduction which is due to extra-focal perception.

A source of error lies in the fact that some figures have a greater attractiveness than others; they become more familiar to the subjects than the less favored figures. An extra-focal glance is sufficient for the perception of such figures, but not for that of unfamiliar figures. As a result the curve does not fall off as steeply as it should. However, it is not without value, and is therefore given.

The abscissas in the accompanying cut give the difference between the point of fixation and the occurrence of the isolated figure. The ordinates give the average ratings of memory for the corresponding experiments.

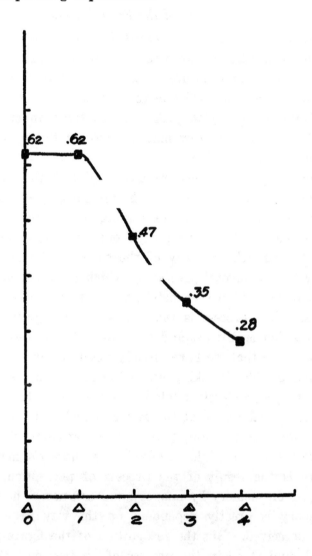

It is evident from the curve that the farther a figure is from the focal point of vision when it is perceived the less accurately it can be reproduced. When it is more than a single space away from the focal point the accuracy of reproduction commences suddenly to decrease.

4. The Process of Recognition.

(a) Analysis of the Experiments.

The experiments that are recorded in this section, though the last to be mentioned, were the first to be made. They are identical in time and nature with those recorded under the heading of Perception. The method is there fully described. It was found necessary to pick out and treat under separate sections that which our raw material offered to us concerning perception and recognition.

In the previous sections we have followed the process of abstraction from its initial stage—the breaking up of the group, —on through the process of perceiving and remembering the common element. We have picked out certain factors which favor and retard the memory of the common element and we come now to that mental process by which the common element is known to have been seen before when it is noticed again in the series. This process is that known as recognition. It is a process which is distinct and separate both in reason and in time from those that we have already described in our analysis of abstraction. The breaking up of the group—perception and memory—are more closely related to one another than to recognition. The breaking up of the group is really an initial stage of perception. Everything perceived is remembered more or less perfectly for a while. Indeed, the subject's memory of the figure is the result of the process of perception, for the experiments on memory by imagery and association have shown that memory is greatly dependent on the way in which the figure is perceived. But the recognition of the figure is a distinct and final stage in the process of abstraction. One need not make many experiments to prove that a figure may be perceived without being recognized. This is witnessed, if witness be necessary, by the subjects' remarking occasionally that early in the experiment they had noted the figure, which finally proved to be the common element. At that time, however, it did not occur to them that this figure was the common element.

There is indeed nothing remarkable in this. But it is somewhat strange that at the close of the experiment subjects would often say that they had seen the figure clearly, two, three or even four times before they stopped the apparatus. Three times seemed to be the usual number. Practice, and strict orders not to wait, did not stop the occurrence of such dilatoriness. This waiting may be due to two things:

(*a*) Time is required for the subject to resolve to stop the apparatus.

(*b*) It often takes an appreciable interval for the process of recognition to develop.

The first may be of importance; the latter certainly is. For in the course of the delay the subjects seem to have a dawning sense that the element in question is the common element. In fact it happened once that the series came to an end while the subject's mind was in this twilight state. He stopped the apparatus and then laughed and said: "Why, it just occurs to me that a figure I have in mind was undoubtedly the common element." There were several other occurrences of the same nature. It seems evident, therefore, that in abstraction there is a process of recognition distinct from the bare perception of the common element. Furthermore, this process of recognition may take an appreciable time for development.

We should expect to find in the process of abstraction a two-fold development, the development of perception and the development of recognition. As there are stages in the process of perception so there should be stages in the process of recognition.

What, then, is to be developed in the process of recognition? From the experiments of this section it is evident that recognition involves something that perception does not involve, namely, the element of certainty or uncertainty. Certainty that the figure has been seen before is what is dawning upon the subject in that state before his mind is fully made up.

If the process of perception were always completed before that of recognition began, our task would be a very simple one. We should have but to add to the stages of perception the various degrees through which the subject goes in arriving at complete certainty, the different shades of probability up to unhesitating assent. But only by accident is the process of perception complete before recognition begins. What happens is that almost any degree of the certainty of recognition may coexist with any degree of the perfection of perception. And this we shall attempt to bring out in the arrangement of our results below. Three main points are picked out in the development of certainty:

The intimation of a common element. At the end of an experiment the subjects were asked to give a description of their mental state during the experiment. The first stage was a kind of inkling that a common element might be present. This stage I have designated as (.1) an Intimation. It is a state of very weak probability and is sometimes due to the presence of similar figures. A more advanced stage I have designated as (2) Probability, and the final stage as (3) Certainty. These divisions of course are arbitrary and flow into each other.

With this explanation the various headings given below will be understood. The numerals in the parentheses show what figure was used as the common element in the experiment in question.[15] This will enable any one to see for himself to what extent the imperfection of perception was due to the complexity of the figure. In some cases at least the complexity of the figure must have been a minor factor. The final state of full recognition with certainty of the fact and a perfect idea of the form has not been put down in the following enumeration of the stages of recognition. It was the more common termination of the experiments and occurred with all subjects.

In order to give a more complete idea of the subject's mind his remarks have been occasionally transcribed and referred to by indices at the right of the numbers which designate the common element of the experiment. These remarks of the subjects, better than any description, give an idea of the course of development.

---

[15] Cf. Fig. 1, p. 118.

It required anywhere from about five to twenty-five exposures for the subject to find the common element. During all these exposures the process of abstraction was in a state of growth and development. Its stages were at first ascertained only by the subject's memory of what occurred during the experiment. Would it not be possible to get a direct observation of these stages by cutting the experiment short, thus giving fewer exposures than the subject ordinarily required? At the end of the experiment the subject would not have finished the process of abstraction; he would not have to recall as well as he could by memory the stages he had noticed in the development of complete certainty. He would simply have to describe by direct introspection his state of mind which would be, at the very moment, in some one of those stages of development.

Simple as the experiment seemed, it was most tantalizing to carry out. Sometimes the subject arrived at complete certainty before the shortened series came to an end. Sometimes the process of abstraction seemed not to have commenced at all, and the subject's mind was in a state of negative doubt.[16] By persistent effort, however, the various stages were confirmed, not all, however, with all subjects. The time necessary for this would have been excessive.. However, a sufficient number of confirmations of the previous results of memory were obtained to make it evident that the stages of development so obtained were no delusions but states of mind that actually occurred. These confirmatory experiments are noted under the same division as the previous ones wherever they were obtained. The words "confirmed by" precede the numbers that refer to the common element of the shortened series.

---

[16] By negative doubt I mean a state of mind in which the subject knows of no evidence either for or against a proposition. In this case the proposition would be: A common element is present on this disk. Positive doubt would occur if one were moved equally by the known evidence for and that against a given proposition.

The Stages of Recognition.

SUBJECT BE.

I. An intimation of a common element, without any knowledge of its form.

(4, 14)-(14, 11)-(7, 10)-(9, 10)-(15, 11)-(9, 13)-(17, 14)-(13, 11)-(14, 11).

II. Probability that a common element is present, but an imperfect idea of the form.

(3, 11)*-(17, 11).

Confirmed by (16, 12)-(5, 9)-(4, 9).

* Subject knew at first that a curved figure was presented.

III. Probability that a common element is present, and a true idea of its form.

Confirmed by (15, 16)-(16, 16).

IV. Certainty that a common element is present, but an imperfect idea of its form.

(10, 14)*-(15, 12)†-(2, 14)-(15, 13)-(11, 13)-(4, 11)‡-(15, 13)-(8, 13)-(9, 11).

* Subject. could not draw figure at all, but was certain that a common element was present.

† Subject was certain that the figure appeared several times, and that it was not one of the ordinary geometrical figures.

‡ Forgot the image of the figure, but was able to find it in the table of figures.

Reaction of the subject to disks with no common element:

(1) Not certain of any common element. But he drew a figure which might perhaps have been common. It was an amalgamation of several similar figures which had occurred on the disk.

(2) Negative doubt.

(3) Negative doubt.

(4) Negative doubt.

(5) Negative doubt.

(6) Inclination to believe that no common element was present.

(7) Very uncertain. If forced to guess one way or the other would say that a common element was present.

(8) More probably no common element was present.

(9) Probably a common element was present. Subject drew as the common element a figure which was a combination of two similar figures that occurred on three disks.

(10) Perhaps a common element was present.

I. An intimation of a common element, without any knowledge of its form.

(7, 10)-(15, 11)-(17, 13)*-(17, 7).

(Confirmed in two cases, but neglected to note what figure was used.)

> * Subject said he was quite certain that for a time he knew a common element was present. What this common element was remained subconscious.

II. Probability that a common element is present, but an imperfect idea of its form.

(4, 14)*-(10, 7)†-(17, 8)-(15, 10).

Confirmed by (5, 9).

> * Thought for a time that a dark spot would turn out to be the common element, as indeed it actually did.
> † The subject was at first conscious of a cloudy flake, which afterwards cleared up.

III. Certainty that a common element is present, but an imperfect idea of its form.

(5, 12)*-(16, 6)†-(14, 10)-(8, 10)-(16, 6)-(10, 7)-(9, 11).

Confirmed by (7, 12).

> * The subject felt conscious of a difference in the size of the figures, and classified them into large and small. At a certain period in the experiment he knew that the common element was not one of the larger figures.
> † The subject knew for a time that the common element was some kind of an unpleasant unsymmetrical figure.

Reaction of the subject to disks with no common element:

(1) Subject stopped the apparatus after twenty-four expositions and said that he noticed no easing of his task as the experiment proceeded. When a common element is present he notices that the process of perception becomes easier as the experiment proceeds.

(2) Nothing noted.

(3) Nothing noted.

(4) Not certain that no common element was present.

(5) Not quite certain that no common element was present.

(6) Almost certain that no common element was present.

(7) More probably no common element present.

(8) Absolute indecision.

(9) Indeterminate.

I. An intimation of a common element, without any knowledge of its form.

This stage was not found with this subject.

II. Probability that a common element is present, but an imperfect idea of its form.

(15, 10)-(10, 10)*-(8, 16)-(4, 13)-(3, 9)†-(4, 9)‡-(16, 8).

> * Wondered for a time whether or not a blurred figure seen out of focal vision was going to turn out to be the common element.
>
> † Subject could describe the figure as symmetrical and oval at one end and said she had a visual image of it; but knew that this visual image was incorrect.
>
> ‡ Probably a funny little figure round at one end, with one line coming to a point.

III. Certainty that a common element is present, but an imperfect idea of its form.

(10, 12)-(10, 16)-(15, 12)-(15, 9).

Reaction of the subject to disks with no common element:

(1) Not sure that no common element was present.

(2) Possibly a tall, slender figure was the common element.

(3) Slight probability of a common element.

(4) Thinks no common element was present.

SUBJECT KR.

I. An intimation of a common element, without any knowledge of its form.

(13, 16)*-(16, 16)-(15, 11)-(15, 10)-(13, 11)-(17, 15)†-(6, 12)-(10, 13)-(4, 13)-(17, 10)‡-(17, 13)‖-(14, 13).

Confirmed by (7, 13).

> * At end of experiment subject drew figure and said he was perfectly certain that it was the common element. Long before he arrived at certainty he had a vague feeling that some kind of a common element was present. Later he knew that it was changing position.
>
> † "Zuerst ein unbestimmtes Gefühl, ohne Object, sehr vag."
>
> ‡ At first a general probability.
>
> ‖ "Increasing feeling of probability, without contents," was an early stage in this experiment.

II. Probability that a common element is present, but an imperfect idea of its form.

(15, 11)*-(4, 13)†-(13, 11).

Confirmed by (16, 13).

> * The subject had at first a feeling that probably a curved figure was the common element.
>
> † A feeling that the common element might be a figure limited by straight lines.

III. Probability that a common element is present, and a true idea of its form.

This stage was found with subject Kr in the series of confirmation experiments with (16, 14).*

> * The image of the figure came to him only after the experiment was over.

IV. Certainty that a common element is present, but an imperfect idea of its form.

(8, 13)-(13, 12)-(16, 6)-(15, 12)-(17, 11).

Reaction of the subject to disks with no common element:

(1) Uncertainty.

(2) Complete uncertainty.

(3) Thinks no common element present.

(4) In first part of experiment a very weak feeling of probability that a common element was present. During about three-fourths of the experiment, an ever increasing probability that no common element was present.

(5) Certainty after 23 expositions that no common element was present.

(6) Very probably no common element.

SUBJECT MO.

I. An intimation of a common element, without any knowledge of its form.

(8, 12)-(11, 12)-(13, 12)-(6, 12)-(3, 13)-(8, 10)*-(12, 14)-(10, 12).

> * There was a first stage of vague probability followed by a blank, and then a rising probability accompanied at first by no definite image.

II. Probability that a common element is present, but an imperfect idea of its form.

(14, 10)*-(14, 15)†-(12, 14)-(10, 12)-(7, 12).‡

> * "There was a time when I thought to myself, 'It is a pointed figure.' "
> † "At first I thought an open kind of figure would be present."
> ‡ There was a time when a strong probability attached itself to some kind of a figure with an angle cut out.

III. Probability that a common element is present, and a true idea of its form.

(12, 13)-(2, 16)*-(4, 12)-(14, 11)-(1, 13).

> * "There was a clearly marked period of doubt during which I thought that a triangular figure was being repeated."

IV. Certainty that a common element is present, but an imperfect idea of its form.

(4, 9).*

> * "For a part of this experiment I knew a figure was being repeated, but I could not catch it. I had very little or no idea of its form."

Reaction of the subject to disks with no common element:

(1) A weak probability that some kind of a common element is present.

(2) A faint probability of a common element with cut-out angles. (A confusion of several figures.)

(3) Faint probability of a common element.

(4) Saw nothing.

(5) Very slight probability of a common element.

(6) Sure that no common element was present.

(7) Very weak probability of a common element.

(8) Negative doubt.

(9) Negative doubt.

(10) Probably no common element present.

(11) Probably no common element present.

SUBJECT R.

I. An intimation of a common element present, without any knowledge of its form.

This stage was not to be found with this subject.

II. Probability that a common element is present, but an imperfect idea of its form.

(12, 14)*-(2, 6)†-(13, 11)-(13, 15).

> * The idea of something like a heart came first; then the thought that it was different from a heart.
> † Noticed at first the outer points.

III. Probability that a common element is present, and a true idea of its form.

(9, 10).

IV. Certainty that a common element is present, but an imperfect idea of its form.

(13, 12)*-(14, 11)-(4, 14)-(2, 6)-(2, 13).†

> * Subject stopped the apparatus before she was sure of the form. There was a time in the experiment when the subject knew that some figure was being repeated, but did not know just what one it was.
> † Saw figure three times. On second exposition she knew that the figure had points and that was all.

Reaction of the subject to disks with no common element:

(1) Nothing noted.

(2) No intimation of a common element.

(3) Probably a common element repeated.

(4) Negative doubt.

(5) Thinks no common element present.

(6) Almost sure that no common element was present.

(7) Thinks no common element present.

SUBJECT W.

I. An intimation of a common element, without any knowledge of its form.

(2, 13)-(13, 3)-(4, 12)*-(17, 13)-(17, 12)†-(17, 13).‡

Confirmed by (12, 15)-(2, 6).

> * Subject saw something changing its position before he could make out its shape.
> † Subject was conscious of a common element all along, but did not know what it was.
> ‡ Subject said he was conscious of a common element before there "really was one present."

II. Probability that a common element is present, but an imperfect idea of its form.

(8, 14)-(8, 12).

Confirmed by (15, 12).*

> * Subject thinks that a common element of angular form was probably the repeated figure.

III. Probability that a common element is present, and a true idea of its form.

(4, 13).

IV. Certainty that a common element is present, but an imperfect idea of its form.

(6, 10)-(12, 14)-(3, 6)-(1, 13).

Confirmed by (14, 13)*-(3, 9).†

> * Subject noticed that the image faded away very rapidly.
> † Subject saw a rounded thing suggesting two points and knew that it was repeated. At end of experiment (10th exposure) he could not draw it. He had a "feeling that it was there before he saw it."

Reaction of the subject to disks with no common element:

(1) Sees nothing.

(2) Thinks none absolutely alike.

(3) Negative doubt.

SUBJECT Z.

I. An intimation of a common element, without any knowledge of its form.

(8, 12)*-(13, 11)-(8, 13)-(4, 14)†-(2, 6)‡-(16, 6)‡-(3, 6)-(2, 13).‖

Confirmed by (15, 14) in two different experiments.

> * At first it seemed to the subject as if a common element was present. Then he looked here and there to find it.
> † At first there was an abstract feeling of something common.
> ‡ First noted something common and new.
> ‖ At first there was an indefinite consciousness of something repeating itself.

II. Certainty that a common element is present, without any knowledge of its form.

(3, 11).

III. Probability that a common element is present, but an imperfect idea of its form.

This stage is not to be found in the records of this subject.

IV. Probability that a common element is present, and a true idea of its form.

(2, 13)-(5, 12)-(10, 10).

Confirmed by (16, 13)-(10, 12).

V. Certainty that a figure is being repeated, but an imperfect idea of its form.

(7, 12)-(13, 11)*-(17, 14).

> * Subject knew that the common element had something round in the middle.

The following observations of this subject are interesting:

(*a*) ''There is no time to compare one figure with another, or one impression with a previous impression.''

(*b*) When a figure was used as a common element which the subject had not seen before, it generally happened that at first he noticed something new and then a special figure.

(*c*) The perception of the common element has a tendency to obliterate the images of the other figures. Before perceiving the common element as common, the images of several figures that have just passed by float about in the mind. When the common element is perceived as such, they vanish at once.

Reaction of the subject to disks with no common element:

(1) Stops apparatus after nine exposures, and says he is perfectly certain that no figure is repeated in each group.

(2) After nine exposures the subject was certain that no common element was present.

(3) Subject thinks that a figure (4, 14) might possibly have been repeated. He drew it correctly along with another figure; which two figures were drawn when he was requested to reproduce everything he could remember as having been seen. This also happened with (17, 15).

(4) No intimation of any figure having been repeated.

(5) No intimation of any figure having been repeated.

(6) Thinks that there was no common element.

(7) State of negative doubt.

(8) Almost certain that no common element was present.

(9) Negative doubt.

(10) Thinks that no common element was present.

(11) Subject thought several times that a common element was present. Then there came an ever increasing certainty that none was present, and at the end of the series he was certain that there was no common element.

Another interesting stage with this subject is that in which the figure on being first noticed is recognized as familiar. By the word familiar, it is not meant that he had seen it before on other disks but that it comes into focal consciousness with a peculiar nuance which tells the subject that this is the common element. It seems that this tone of familiarity (*Bekanntheitsqualität*) arises from the figure's being seen before but not analyzed out from the other figures.

The subject whose results are about to be recounted could give by introspection at the end of the experiment no information at all about the development of the mental process he had just experienced. When later on in the semester I commenced to confirm the results of self-observation, I tried the same method with this subject. I cut the experiment short after he had seen fifteen groups of figures and then asked him simply: "What do you think? Is there a common element present or not? Are you certain or merely inclined more or less to think that you see a common element? Draw what you remember!" In this way was obtained what the subject's introspective memory failed to reveal. Cross-sections were obtained in the course of development and fixed before they could fade from memory.

SUBJECT U.

I. An intimation of a common element, without any knowledge of its form.

(5, 12)-(7, 13)-(10, 9)-(10, 12).

II. Probability that a common element is present, but an imperfect idea of its form.

(2, 6)-(17, 15)-(16, 13)-(4, 9)-(2, 12).

III. Probability that a common element is present, and a true idea of its form.

This stage was not found with this subject.

IV. Certainty that a common element is present, but an imperfect idea of its form.

(10, 7)-(4, 14)-(8, 10)-(10, 6)*-(5, 9).

* Certain only that he had seen the "two eyes" recur.

Reaction of the subject to disks with no common element:

(1) No idea of any common element at the end of the experiment.

(2) No idea of any common element at the end of the experiment.

(3) Complete uncertainty at end of experiment.

(4) No idea of any common element at the end of the experiment.

(5) No common element noted.

(b) Interpretation of the Results.

(i) The Immediate Experimental Conclusions.

When we look at these results it becomes at once apparent that an element of certainty and uncertainty is involved in the process of recognition. If we ask ourselves what this means. we must say that whenever the mind is certain of anything, it assents; and whenever we have an assent we have an act of judgment. One of the immediate empirical conclusions of our results may be stated thus: *The process of recognition involves an element of certainty or uncertainty.*

From this we may conclude: *That the process of recognition involves a judgment or a suspended judgment.* For whenever I am certain I assent; and whenever my mind is in a state of uncertainty, assent is suspended. In the one case there is a judgment; in the other, judgment is suspended. It is not necessary that this judgment should be formulated in so many words. In fact, one may venture to say that in most cases of perfect recognition there is no verbal formulation of the judgment at all; but the psychological act of judging is nevertheless really and truly present.

The presence of a judgment in the act of recognition proves that the act of perception which does not involve a judgment is an essentially different and less highly developed mental state. Recognition is indeed a perception, and over and above this a judgment is passed upon the perception. This judgment involves the statement that what is now perceived has been perceived before. If recognition is incomplete the judgment hangs in suspense and cannot be definitely passed.

In the further study of recognition we have only to ask ourselves, what is the basis of this judgment? Do the experiments help us out?

If we run through the results we will find that any degree of certainty may be accompanied by any degree of the perfection of perception. A person can be certain that a figure was repeated and have a perfect image of the figure, or an imperfect image, or no image at all. A second empirical conclusion may be stated thus: *Assured recognition is not dependent upon perfect perception.* And why this statement? Simply because it is an empirical fact that assured recognition can exist with a very imperfect perception,—a perception that is so imperfect that it involves no mental image whatsoever.[17]

While indeed we have not found out, as yet, on what the judgment of recognition depends, we have at least discovered something on which it does not depend. And that is the mental image. This suffices finally to dispose of one theory of recognition, now generally rejected by psychologists—the theory, namely, that recognition is brought about by the comparison of the present sensation with a revived mental image. Identity being perceived, the object seen is then recognized. That such a comparison of images is unnecessary appears from the experiments. Why? Because recognition takes place not only when there is no revived mental image of the past perception, but when the present perception itself is too imperfect to leave any trace of mental imagery in the mind. Recognition, however, may take place by a comparison of mental images. In general the rapidity of succeeding impressions made this an impossible, or at least a very awkward, process. It once hap-

---

[17] Cf. also above, pp. 134-136.

pened, however, that a subject reported that she had used just this methdd in arriving at certainty of recognition. On thinking that she had seen a certain figure twice, she tried to call up the previous image that she had in mind as identical with the figure just seen, and institute a comparison between the two images. However we must note that *recognition was already in the probable stage* when this was done. And the *comparison* that was attempted was after all only *an auxiliary method.*

The comparison of images, therefore, may come in as an aid, but it is not necessary to recognition nor is it the normal method. One might object to the use of the word 'normal' here as carrying us beyond the limits of legitimate deduction. Was not the rapidity with which the exposures succeeded one another expressly chosen to exclude the possibility of comparing mental images? That is true, and our experiments prove only that the comparison of mental images is not necessary in the process of recognition. As to its being the normal method, we can from our own experiments only conjecture. But there are other experiments along this line. I refer to those on the recognition of the identity of time intervals, tones, etc. When a subject listens to two raps separated by a short interval, and then, after a period of waiting, hears two more raps, how is it that he recognizes that the second two raps mark off an interval of time equal to that of the first? Does he really compare some kind of mental images of the two time intervals? It would seem from the experimental research on this point, that he does not.[18]

Professor Frank Angell has made it abundantly clear that the recognition of tones does not depend on a comparison of mental images. In his study of the "Discrimination of Clangs for Different Intervals of Time," he arrived at the following results:

"The main conclusion to be drawn from the distraction experiments is that judgments of tone discriminations can take place, and in the majority of our experiments did take place,

---

[18] Cf. Wundt, *Physiologische Psychologie*, III, 5, 476-517.

without conscious comparison between the present sensation and a memory-image of a past sensation. When, for example, a reagent, after a long time-interval filled with interesting reading, from which he had to be practically aroused by a sharp signal in order to prepare himself for the apprehension of the second tone, nevertheless delivered a judgment with a feeling of considerable security, it is idle to speak of "memory-images" or indeed of comparison in the ordinary meaning of the word. Or when a reagent, after having accurately discriminated six pairs of tones, decided with ease that a tone just given is like or unlike a tone 4 vibrations higher or lower sounded 60 seconds before, and is correct in these decisions 63 times in 100, it is evident that the ordinary theories of tone-comparisons need readjustment.

"No more is it explicable on the theory of memory comparison that there should not have been a great increase in doubtful judgments in passing from undistracted to distracted discrimination, or indeed in failures to judge at all, or that the several forms of distraction should not have shown a far greater difference in effect than was actually the case."[19]

In the light, then, of our experiments, and also those on the recognition of various sensory stimuli, it is not too much to say that the comparison of mental images is not the normal method of recognition.

Summing up, then, the conclusions that we may regard as established by the experiments of this section we may state:

A. The process of recognition involves an element of certainty or uncertainty. From this follows:

The process of recognition involves a judgment or a suspended judgment.

B. Certain recognition is not dependent on perfect perception. From this it was seen to follow that:

A comparison of mental images is not necessary to the process of recognition.

---

[19] *Amer. Journ. Psychol.*, 12, 1900-1901, p. 69.

An empirical fact rather than a conclusion from these experiments is stated in the following proposition:

Certain recognition can take place without the formation of any mental image of the thing that is recognized.[20]

(ii) THE BASIS OF JUDGMENT IN RECOGNITION.

When we are asked to give an account of the real basis of judgment in recognition we naturally ask, how is the object that is recognized remembered? The factors of memory, one might suppose, are active to a large extent in the process of recognition. We are naturally concerned with the factors which enabled the subjects to memorize the figures used in our experiments which represented rather complex conditions. It cannot be taken for granted that the basis of recognition is the same for simple sensations and complex perceptions. In fact it is rather likely that what serves as our cue in one case does not meet the demands of another, that what is the chief basis of recognition of a simple tone may become a very minor factor in the recognition of a time-interval. And what is prominent in recognizing a time-interval may become subordinate in the recognition of a street or a house as places where one has been before. On this account it is desirable to take for experiment such complex material as our figures, in order to see if any factors enter into the process of recognition that have not been noticed in the usual experiments on time-intervals, colors, tones, etc.

The process by which the figures are remembered should give us some clue to the method used in their recognition. In the section entitled, ''The Factor of Memory in the Process of Abstraction'' (p. 139), we compared memory by visualization and by motor imagery, with memory by association and analysis. A marked advantage was found in favor of the latter. Memory by association consisted in relating the figure to known objects, or analyzing it and thus relating it to certain mental categories. These mental categories are the

---

[20] This conclusion is based in great part upon the experiments given on pp. 134 ff.

bonds which hold the figure in place and make possible its recall when it has left the field of consciousness. In fact, it seems that if all the conceptual ties could be cut, or be lacking from the beginning, the figure would fade away completely and recall would be impossible. We find also that, in the process of perception, the essential element is not the formation of a visual image but the relating of the object perceived to one or more mental categories. Nor must we regard this relating of the impression of an object to its categories as a manipulation of separate and distinct psychical entities. It is rather what Wundt would call an assimilation. The sensation and the general concepts form a psychical compound which differs from its elements and is a new mental product. What are the elements of this compound? Wundt speaks of the feelings involved, especially that of familiarity, the sensation and the images to which it is assimilated. But we may question the completeness of this analysis.

There seems to be something that is not included therein and that something lies in the mental categories that couple the perception of the object to the train of memory. These, the essential elements of assimilation in perception, are also the elements *par excellence* of recognition. An assimilation does take place, and on the basis of our experiments on memory and the analysis of perception we may venture to say that the chief elements of assimilation are the concepts to which the sensations are assimilated in the process of perception. When the figure is seen it is at once assimilated to certain mental categories; it is regarded as made of straight or curved lines; it has elements that curve; it is an open or a dark figure; it is symmetrical and regular, or just the reverse. These phrases do not stand for images that are present; this the cases of recognition without imagery prove. But suppose they do so stand; suppose we have in recognition an assimilation of a present sensation to a number of revived images—of lines, curves, points, etc. Certainly the new psychical product should be an image, a product of the sensation and the imagery of past experience. But there were cases in which recognition took place without the trace of an image. Consequently the assimilation would appear to be of elements that are not images. These elements we may speak of as mental categories or concepts. The sensation of a figure never stands alone. Perhaps no sensation ever does. It is related to an appropriate series of concepts. These are not all in focal consciousness. Perhaps all remain unanalyzed in the background of consciousness until by reflection we consider what kind of a figure we have seen. But the sensation plus the concepts with which it is associated,—these are assimilated and constitute a new psychical product. This psychical product is what is known as our 'idea' of the figure. My subjects have sometimes said: "I have an idea of what the figure is, but I cannot draw it." And then after some thought they would give a very inadequate description which would relate the figure to some concept. On being allowed to look for the figure they would find it among the entire lot of figures that made up our material. Our 'idea' of the figure is whatever image may be present plus the concepts to which it is assimilated. *That which is the chief factor in perception, that by which we recall figures, is also that by which we recognize them.* And this is the figure's series of associated concepts. When a figure is seen once, some kind of an 'idea' of the figure is formed—it is fitted in to one or more mental categories. When it is seen again the new percept is assimilated to the old. The old series of associated concepts falls in with the new. And in this way, perhaps, is produced the tone of familiarity. In the process of assimilation there is nothing that jars; on the contrary there is a reinforcement at least of some members of the associated train of concepts. New concepts may be brought out, but they fit in with the old. Merely similar figures, however, might on a later perception bring out new concepts which would contradict the old and thereby destroy the feeling of familiarity and give rise to doubt as to the identity of the figures.

One who is not disposed to give such individuality to the concept as distinct from sensation and mental imagery might have recourse, as Wundt does, to the feelings. When we find no image in the process of recognition we must not jump to a conclusion that a concept distinct from our mental imagery is present. There are the feelings to be taken into consideration. Perhaps these mental categories are groups of feelings and not a class of mental states by themselves. ˉ The examination of this point leads us to our next chapter, in which we analyze the product of abstraction.

IV.

THE PRODUCT OF THE PROCESS OF ABSTRACTION.

In our analysis of the process by which an abstraction is formed, we have necessarily learned something about the final product. We have watched the growth of a complex mental state and must necessarily know something about that mental state in its final stage. Are there any evident elements in the final product of abstraction that we may regard as facts of experience? Yes. Our experiments have revealed some to which we called attention in our section on the process of perception. From the results of that section, confirmed as they are by the succeeding chapters, there are two important facts that were abundantly evident.

(a) *There exist imageless mental contents representative of a visible object.* Our own experiments are not the only evidence on this point. A reference to the history of the problem[1] will show that a number of psychologists have determined the existence of various kinds of imageless mental contents. The consensus of evidence is such that 'thoughts' without imagery must be looked upon as established mental facts. And when we take perception to mean the result of the process of perception, our experiments show conclusively that we can have a perception of a visible object in which there is no visual imagery. Our idea of that visual object is therefore not a mental picture, although under such conditions as obtained in our experiments we should expect, if at all, to find visual imagery constantly developed.

Without, however, making any assumption as to the nature of these imageless mental contents we may regard their existence as an established fact. They are the essential elements in the product of perception and abstraction. The existence of any

---

[1] Cf. pp. 76 ff.

kind of mental imagery in the complex product is not essential. Imageless mental content and not imagery is therefore the true product of abstraction.

'The second fact of experiment is this: (*b*) *Perception is a process of assimilating the data of sense experience to their appropriate mental categories.* By this assimilation the object is perceived. The word category is not here taken in any pre-conceived sense. It is a fact that in perceiving a figure the earlier stages were designated as a knowledge that the figure was "pointed" or "open" or "round" or "had the top lines crossed," etc. These expressions are examples of what I mean here by categories. It is a fact, too, that these expressions were not descriptions of mental images. The figures, however, had been seen with the eyes, and in perceiving them they were inter-preted in terms of the previous knowledge of the subject. This I have expressed by saying that the figures were assimilated to appropriate mental categories. So far this is all that I mean by the word category.

Let us now ask, what are these mental categories in terms of our modern psychological terminology? A current psycho-logical division of our mental states leaves room for nothing but (*a*) sensations and their images, (*b*) feelings, and (*c*) will, which by some psychologists is explained in terms of feeling. To these states and combinations of them many psychologists have attempted to reduce our mental processes. We may now ask ourselves to which of these classes do the mental categories of perception belong?

(1) Do they belong to the class of sensations and images?

The 'mental categories' are not, of course, sensations, and we have already shown that they can not be directly interpreted as images, because they exist without imagery. Dr. Ach, how-ever, has a theory[2] by which they might be the combined effect of many images. They are not images but the tendencies of a whole host of images to reproduce themselves. This theory was excogitated to explain the meaning of words. A word is

---

[2] Cf. above, p. 86.

understood because it sets a number of images in readiness, all of which have a tendency to reproduce themselves. This tendency of the images to reproduce themselves is the meaning of the word.

Against this as a theory of the meaning of words one may object:

(*a*) If a single image can not constitute a meaning it is hard to see how the tendency of a whole host of meaningless images to come into consciousness would constitute a meaning.

(*b*) If we refer to the section in the experiments of Bühler[3] entitled ''Ueber das Auffassen von Gedanken'' we will see that the 'mental categories' which were used by his subjects in the understanding of sentences cannot be analyzed into any known form of mental imagery.

(*c*) Furthermore, words express objects for which we can have no adequate imagery. How then can the mere tendency of this inadequate imagery to reproduce itself constitute the meaning of the word?

The same objections which prevent our acceptance of Ach's theory as an explanation of the meaning of words preclude its application to the 'mental categories' of our own experiments.

It would explain meaning by the tendency of meaningless mental contents to reproduce themselves; for pure sensation independent of its associations has no meaning; neither has an image. It must be associated with other mental states to be understood. If these mental states are themselves but a host of images, each one of which has no significance in itself, from their combinations we can not bring about meaning. Nor can this tendency to appear in consciousness be said to constitute meaning. For the mere tendency of meaningless mental states to appear in consciousness would give no meaning that was not in these states themselves.

One might challenge the statement that pure sensations or mental images independent of their associations have no meaning. Let us therefore develop this point a little further.

---

[3] *Archiv für die ges. Psychol.*, 12, pp. 12 ff.

Whatever may be our theory, it is a fact that a complex of— sensations on being received into the mind *is* interpreted. This is evident from our section on perception. The interpretation takes place by means of the something that we may term 'mental categories,' to which the sensation is associated. These give it a meaning. But suppose the sensation is not assimilated to these mental categories? Is this not merely to say that it is not understood and has no meaning? What is left to meaning when you deprive it of every possible association and every mental category into which it might be resolved? It dwindles to nothing and ceases to be meaning.

These mental categories possess meaning by their own right and are qualitatively distinct from sensations and images.

One might bring in at this point Ribot's 'intentional' theory of the mental image.[4] Sensations and mental images are signs of their objects. But as we said in our passing criticism of Ribot, if the mental image is a sign of the object that it represents, it must be understood. On one side of the sign is the object signified, on the other is the meaning of the sign. If the mental image is a sign it must not only have an object but also a meaning. Consequently, to say that the image is a sign does not help us to get along without any kind of an idea or concept which functions as a meaning. If, therefore, by acting as a sign sensations and mental images cannot account for meaning, if they themselves are not the meaning, we must seek for meaning elsewhere than in sensations and their mental images.

However, if we could take Dr. Ach's *"Vorstellung"* in the sense of a mental 'concept with meaning' we have in the theory a good analysis of a number of those states which Marbe and his followers have termed *"Bewusstseinslagen."*[5] They are mental states in which several concepts tend to appear in consciousness—but no one succeeds in doing so. As a result, you have a more or less unanalyzable mental state without definite

---

4 Cf. above, pp. 78 ff.

5 Cf. above, p. 85.

characteristic. The tendency of the many 'concepts with meaning' to appear in consciousness results in an imageless mental content, which is hard to characterize, simply because many characteristics tend to come before the mind but no one succeeds in doing so.

(2) Are the 'mental categories' feelings?

Those who hold to the opinion that feelings of pleasure and pain constitute the sole elements of our emotional life will not be disposed to seek in these affective states an interpretation of our 'mental categories.' These 'mental categories' express knowledge; and knowledge is not pleasure and pain, though it may be pleasurable or painful. Nor does it make any difference how we may extend the idea of feeling; if we still mean by it something that is not knowledge, then thoughts and 'mental categories' can never be explained in terms of feeling. For if the word 'feelings' remains an exact scientific term to designate those very mental processes which do not give us knowledge, if feeling is opposed to sensation and to all our cognitive mental processes, then the 'mental categories' we have defined above are not states of feeling.

Such considerations as these could hardly have escaped Wundt. Yet he would interpret our 'thoughts,' and I suppose what I have termed 'mental categories,' as a complex of images and the "adequate" feelings which are involved. Our 'mental categories,' he claims, are not feelings alone and not images alone, but a complex of both. But if imagery is in itself meaningless, if we can have 'thoughts' which are not images, then the representative function of our thoughts and 'mental categories' must be performed by the 'feelings.' No single individual can place a limit to the meaning of a term. Thorndike calls every single one of our mental processes a 'feeling.' To this even Wundt would object. Still, if he were to insist on embracing under the term 'feelings' the representative content of our thoughts as well as their affective tone, he should at least admit that there are two very distinct classes of feeling —one which gives the affective tone and another which represents the object. Wundt has nowhere made this admission. In fact, from his writings it would seem that the representative function is ascribed by him to the imagery in the complex mental content termed a 'thought.' But on being accused of this by Bühler he strenuously objected that Bühler had not read his works[6] and maintained that in his analysis of thought there was also the concept of the feelings. Consequently, the question arises: Do these feelings represent the object or not? If not, they can never account for the representative function of 'thought.' If they do, then surely we must classify our feelings into those that represent an object and those that do not; for it is certainly clear that there exists a large class of feelings which are not representative of objects.

If then there are 'feelings' which can represent an object, how, we may ask, does this come about? How in the absence of imagery, and independent of it, can any combination of Wundt's entire tri-dimensional system of feelings account for the meaning of words and phrases or the mental categories formed in the perception of our figures? Pleasure and pain, tension and relaxation, excitement and repose, might conceivably combine to form complex emotions, moods, and a variety of non-representative mental states which accompany our processes of recognition, abstraction, analysis, etc. But that they should take over in their combination a function which is qualitatively distinct from any that is inherent in them as elements, is an unwarrantable assumption.

One might bring forward at this point the following objection: Your contention that there exist imageless mental contents is based in great measure on the experiments in which a common element was certainly perceived, although the subject did not at all know precisely what kind of a figure was present. But to conclude from such experiments that imageless ideas exist is not warranted, because the experiments may be explained without such an assumption. These experiments represent those cases in which the common element was never seen in the focal

---

[6] *Psychol. Studien*, 3, pp. 347-348 (note).

point of consciousness. But wherever it was perceived, however far in the background it might be, it gave rise to certain feelings of relaxation and restfulness, perhaps even of pleasure or displeasure. The peculiar combination of these feelings gave rise to the feeling of certainty that a figure was being repeated. This feeling had connected with it no visual imagery that the subject could recall. From such an analysis it is evident that from the lack of mental imagery you can not jump to the conclusion that there are imageless concepts.

Such an objection would not be based upon a complete analysis of the evidence. The existence of imageless concepts is not founded solely upon these rare cases—but also upon cases in which the subject was certain of parts of the figure that could easily have been drawn had any visual imagery been present. The subject described things such as points or curves or angles, which certainly could be pictured, but claimed to have no picture and could draw nothing that would represent his state of mind. Now, points and angles and curves are not mere feelings. And if they are present to the mind without imagery they are not images.

Furthermore, in the cases of recognition of figures without any knowledge whatsoever of their special nature, it is perfectly true that the basis of the subject's judgment to a large extent was some combination of feelings such as was mentioned in the supposed objection. But we must not forget that the basis of a judgment is not the judgment itself. And we must also remember that in all these cases there is in the subject's mind the abstraction, 'some kind of a figure' plus the knowledge that 'the figure was repeated.' The knowledge expressed by these two terms constitutes the judgment, 'some kind of a figure was repeated.' This judgment is not constituted by the feelings which evidenced the presence of a figure. It is based upon them, but it does not consist in them. It is therefore something over and above them. The elements into which this judgment can be analyzed are the abstraction 'some kind of a figure' and the knowledge that it 'was repeated.'

Since these elements are not feelings and are not mental
images, there is nothing left in the current division of elementary mental processes into which they can be relegated except
the acts of will. But certainly we can not place them there.
We must therefore recognize the existence of another division
of mental processes to which our thoughts and mental categories
must be relegated. Consequently in the final product of ab-—
straction there is an element distinct from imagery and feelings.
This element, since it is the bearer of the meaning, is the kernel
of the product and it may truly be termed the 'thought' or the
'concept.' Imagery and feeling may cluster about this concept;
but as far as the imagery is concerned it is certainly lacking
at times, as our experiments have shown. As to feeling, we
can not say for certain on the basis of our experiments whether
or not it is necessarily present.

The concept of the figures in our experiments, though distinct from imagery and feeling, was not itself an elementary
process. It was manifestly compound in a number of instances.
For one and the same figure was assimilated to several mental
categories. It was a concept made up of several more elementary
concepts. Between the concepts of which it was constituted
there was a conscious bond. The sensation in being assimilated—
picked out its categories by the necessary process of its assimilation and these united to form a concept of the figure which
the subject was afterwards enabled to analyze with more or less
completeness.

If such is the case one may ask how was the first concept
formed? Does man come into the world equipped with a whole
system of mental categories by which he is enabled to perceive
and understand the things about him? This question leads us
on into a problem far beyond the limits of the present research.
Our problem has been the analysis of the process of abstraction
in the adult. The process of perception which is the initial
stage of abstraction was found to be one of assimilating the
sensation to previously formed mental categories. Whence
originated these mental categories, is another problem. These

mental categories and their function in perception are facts. The origin of the mental categories, and the process of perception and abstraction in the child, are very different problems from our own. But ignorance of child psychology does not destroy the facts of adult mental life.

However, it may not be out of place to suggest a theory as to the origin of our mental categories. And this I would do as follows: As Külpe suggests,[7] the data of sense are perceived. There exists something of the nature of an 'inner sense'—a central consciousness which perceives the phenomena of the external senses. When consciousness first dawns the data of external sensations are perceived. Perhaps at first in the automatic life of the child the sensations that are perceived are more or less intermittent and vary in their nature. But every time a sensation arouses consciousness the child is aware of a change in its mental life. At first this change is not interpreted because there are as yet no mental categories. Every change is just an awareness. The child simply realizes that something has happened. And this realization develops into his first mental category. As time goes on, experiences multiply and the several different kinds of experiences make the child not only aware that 'something has happened' but that something of a more particular nature has happened. Something painful, something pleasant—something hot or something cold, etc. In this way he forms still further sets of mental categories into which his future experience is received. Out of these develop the categories of identity and diversity,—when, we do not know; nor is it necessary for us to settle this point here. But by a gradual determination of the most general of his mental categories—'something'—his experience grows and is assimilated. The first determinations are of very particular experiences. The most varied things are given one and the same name, simply because he has but a few general concepts and his sensations are assimilated by necessity to whatever categories may have been developed. The child's experience—his inner perception of a train

---

[7] *Bericht ü. d. I. Kongress f. exp. Psychol. in Giessen, 1904*, p. 67.

of similar mental events constitute a mental category which is his idea of those events. The first mental category, the child's awareness of something, enters though not consciously and explicitly into all his later concepts. Some of these later ones group together, and so on, until under the influence of language and education the events of the external world receive their interpretation.

SUMMARY.

We are now in a position to summarize the process of abstraction as revealed in our experiments.

1. The process of abstraction is initiated by the breaking up of the group presented for perception. In this breaking up of the group the common element becomes accentuated at the expense of the surrounding elements. These are not merely neglected, but are positively cast aside and swept more or less completely from the field of consciousness.

2. This breaking up of the group initiates the process of perceiving the common element. This is accomplished by assimilating to known mental categories the sensations perceived. Perception proceeds from that which is more general to that which is particular. The formation of a reproducible image represents a later and unessential stage of perception.

3. The retention in memory of the figure perceived depends in great measure on the method of memory. Memory by analysis and association has a very decided advantage over memory by imagery. The memory of the figure depends, furthermore, upon the focality of perception. The accuracy of memory decreases rapidly with the distance of the figure from the focal point in the act of vision by which it was perceived. The perception of new groups after a figure has been perceived has a tendency to obliterate it from memory.

4. The recognition of a figure once seen involves an element of certainty or uncertainty. Consequently there is implied in recognition assent or doubt, and therefore a judgment or a suspended judgment. In recognizing a figure any degree of certainty of recognition can accompany any degree of perfection in the perception of a figure, so that a subject may be certain of the repetition of a figure and still may have no knowledge as to what manner of figure it was—or the subject may know

all about a given figure and simply draw it as remembered, or as very doubtfully the common element.

5. The final product of abstraction, that which is perceived as common to many groups, is essentially a concept distinct from imagery and feeling. It is not an elementary concept, but represents the assimilation of that which is perceived by the senses to a more or less complex mental category, or perhaps to several such categories. These mental categories may be regarded as the results of past experience.

REFERENCES.*

ACH, NARZISS: *Ueber Willenstätigkeit und das Denken.* Göttingen, 1905.

ANGELL and HARWOOD: "Discrimination of Clangs for Different Intervals of Time." Part I, *American Journal of Psychology,* 1899-1900, Vol. XI, pp. 67-79. Part II, by Prof. Angell alone. *Op. cit.,* Vol. XII, pp. 58-79.

ASTER, E. VON: "Die psychologische Beobachtung und experimentelle Untersuchung von Denkvorgängen." *Zeitschrift für Psychologie,* 1908, Vol. XLIX, pp. 56-107.

BAGLEY, WILLIAM CHANDLER: "The Apperception of the Spoken Sentence." *American Journal of Psychology,* 1900-01, Vol. XII, pp. 80-134.

BERKELEY, GEORGE: *A Treatise concerning the Principles of Human Knowledge.* Vol. I, Fraser's, Oxford (1871) Edition of his works.

BIGHAM, JOHN: "Memory." *Psychological Review,* 1894, Vol. I, pp. 453-461.

BINET, ALFRED: *L'Etude expérimentale de l'intelligence.* Paris, 1903.

BÜHLER, KARL: "Tatsachen und Probleme zu einer Psychologie der Denkvorgänge." *Archiv für die ges. Psychologie,* 1907, Vol. IX, pp. 297-365; 1908, Vol. XII, pp. 1-92.

——— ———: "Antwort auf die von W. Wundt erhobenen Einwände." *Archiv für die ges. Psychologie,* 1908, Vol. XII, pp. 93-123.

——— ———: "Zur Kritik der Denkexperimente." *Zeitschrift für Psychologie,* 1909, Vol. LI, pp. 108-118.

DAVIES, ARTHUR ERNEST: "An Analysis of Psychic Process." *Psychological Review,* 1905, Vol. XII, pp. 166-206.

DÜRR, E.: "Ueber die experimentelle Untersuchung der Denkvorgänge" *Zeitschrift für Psychologie,* 1908, Vol. XLIX, pp. 313-340.

GALTON, FRANCIS: "Composite portraits made by combining those of many different persons into a single resultant figure." *The Journal of the Anthropological Institute of Great Britain and Ireland,* 1879, Vol. VIII, pp. 132-144.

——— ———: "Generic Images." *Proceedings of the Royal Institute of Great Britain,* 1879, pp. 161-171.

——— ———: *Inquiries into Human Faculty,* New York, 1883.

GRÜNBAUM, A. A.: "Ueber die Abstraktion der Gleichheit." *Archiv für die ges. Psychologie,* 1908, Vol. XII, pp. 340-478.

HUXLEY, THOMAS H.: *David Hume,* New York, 1879.

---

* The list is not a bibliography of the subject but contains merely those works referred to in the present study.

KÜLPE, O.: "Versuche über Abstraktion." *Bericht über den I Kongress für experimentelle Psychologie in Giessen,* 1904, pp. 56-68.

MARRE, K.: *Experimentell-psychologische Untersuchungen über das Urteil.* Leipzig, 1901.

MAYER und ORTH: "Zur qualitativen Untersuchungen der Association." *Zeitschrift für Psychologie,* 1901, Vol. XXVI, pp. 1-13.

MESSER, AUGUST: "Experimentell-psychologische Untersuchungen über das Denken." *Archiv für die ges. Psychologie,* 1906, Vol. VIII, pp. 1-224.

——— ———: "Bemerkungen zu meiner 'Experimentell-psychologischen Untersuchungen über das Denken." *Archiv für die ges. Psychologie,* 1907, Vol. X, pp. 409-428.

MEUMANN, E.: "Ueber Associationsexperimente mit Beeinflussung der Reproduktionszeit." *Archiv für die ges. Psychologie,* 1907, Vol. IX, pp. 117-150.

MITTENZWEI, KUNO: "Ueber abstrahierende Apperzeption." *Psychol. Studien,* 1906-07, Vol. II, pp. 358-492.

MOORE, T. V.: "The Process of Recognition." *Atti del V. Congresso internazionale di Psicologia, tenuto in Roma dal 26 al 30 Aprile, 1905,* Roma, 1906, pp. 286-287.

ORTH, JOHANNES: "Gefühl und Bewusstseinslage." *Sammlung von Abhundlungen aus dem Gebiete der Pädagogischen Psychol. und Physiologie.* Edited by Ziegler and Ziehen, Vol. VI, No. 4, Berlin, 1903.

RIBOT, TH.: "Enquête sur les idées générales." *Revue philosophique,* 1891, Vol. XXXII, pp. 376, 388.

——— ———: *L'Evolution des idées générales.* Paris, 1897.

SCHULTZE, F. E. OTTO "Einige Hauptgesichtspunkte der Beschreibung in der Elementarpsychologie. I. Erscheinungen und Gedanken." *Archiv für die ges. Psychologie,* 1906, Vol. VIII, pp. 241-338.

——— ———: "Beitrag zur Psychologie des Zeitbeweisstseins." *Archiv für die ges. Psychologie,* 1908, Vol. XIII, pp. 275-351.

SPEARMANN, C.: "The Proof and Measurement of Association between Two Things." *American Journal of Psychology,* 1904, Vol. XV, pp. 72-101.

TAYLOR, CLIFTON O.: "Ueber das Verstehen von Worten und Sätzen." *Zeitschrift für Psychologie,* 1906, Vol. XL, pp. 225-251.

WATT, HENRY J.: "Experimentelle Beiträge zu einer Theorie des Denkens." *Archiv für die ges. Psychologie,* 1905, Vol. IV, pp. 289-436.

WILTSE, S. E.: "Observations on General Terms." *Am. Journal of Psychology,* 1890-91, III, pp. 144-148.

WUNDT, WILHELM: *Grundzüge der physiologischen Psychologie.* 5th Edition, Leipzig, 1902-03.

——— ———: "Ueber Ausfrageexperimente und über die Methoden zur Psychologie des Denkens." *Psychologische Studien,* 1907, Vol. III, pp. 301-360.

——— ———: "Kritische Nachlese zur Ausfragemethode." *Archiv für die ges. Psychologie,* 1908, Vol. XI, pp. 444-459.

APPENDIX I.

THE INFLUENCE OF ASSOCIATION ON PERCEPTION.

In the course of the experiments a number of cases occurred in which the subject's drawing of the common element differed from the actual figure in such a way that the error was evidently due to the association that was reported. Some of these cases are given below. The drawings given under the heading "subject's drawing" reproduce the essential characters of those made by the observer. They are not however exact reproductions of his drawings.

COMMON ELEMENT.	SUBJECT'S DRAWING.	ASSOCIATION.
▱	 ∞	"Wurst."
Ω	Ω	Omega.
🛢	The subject drew the figure correctly at first. He then changed his mind and drew a second figure with a 🛢 double curve, saying that this was more correct.  He said the figure looked like a (*Läufer*). His second figure does in fact resemble the bishop in some forms of chessmen.	
Ω	 �	Mushroom.
 ⋈	)(	Two half-moons.
 ⋈	 ✂	Open scissors.
 ♡	 ♉	Apple.

These errors lend additional evidence to the theory of perception advanced in the body of this work. The actual imagery arising from the figure itself is not the first thing noticed. It fits into and is interpreted in the light of the subject's past experience. The association comes into the subject's mind first. He sees *that*, and interprets the data of vision in its light before the true image is perceived. Had the series in which these errors occurred been sufficiently long there can be no doubt but that the error of assimilation would have been corrected. The true image which was constantly being impressed upon the retina would have eventually been noticed as it was in itself. But because perception does not consist in merely seeing with one's eyes but in interpreting the data of the senses, such errors as the above are not only possible but natural.

APPENDIX II.

GENERIC IMAGES.

What looked like a fusion of mental images occurred twice in the course of the experiments. Such fusions are interesting in view of the generic image theory of ideas. The first case was less evidently one of fusion. The disk was inaccurately made. The accompanying figure occurred as the common element, now in one, now in another of the two positions as given.

The result was that the two circles were drawn correctly. Just what was in the inner one remained doubtful.

The second case seemed evidently a fusion of mental images. It occurred on a disk with no common element. The accom-

panying two figures occurred several expositions apart. The subject drew the common element. The outline he said was subject drew ⚠ as the common element. The outline he said was certain, the dotted inner line was doubtful. Since the two figures appeared several expositions apart there can be no question at all of a retinal fusion. The phenomenon must be due to some central cause.

Just such cases as these resemble very closely those postulated by the Huxley-Galton theory of general ideas. The common features are deeply impressed and therefore retained; the variable, but faintly, and are neglected. There is however a very important difference between the universal idea and such "generic images," as were found in the entire course of the experiments.

In the formation of a general idea there is a kernel picked out as constantly recurring and therefore essential, while that which is variable is neglected and forgotten, or recognized as unessential.

If in our experiments there was any fusion of images at all, that which was common was indeed clearly impressed,—but that which was variable was neither neglected nor forgotten but remained obscure and doubtful.

At all events the extreme rarity of the phenomenon postulated by the Huxley-Galton theory shows that it cannot be the usual way in which we form our concepts,—not even those of sensible objects. The analysis of abstraction made possible by the experiments points to a process that has little to do with composite photography.

Transmitted December, 1909.

LB Ja '13

UNIVERSITY OF CALIFORNIA PUBLICA

ZOOLOGY.—W. E. Ritter and Charles A. Kofoid, Ed
umes I (pp. 317), II (pp. 382), III (pp. 383),
pleted. Volumes VI and VII in progress. Con
contains the Contributions from the Laboratory
of San Diego.

MEMOIRS OF THE UNIVERSITY OF CALIFORNI
Vol. 1. No. 1. Triassic Ichthyosauria, with speci
Forms. By John C. Merriam. Pag
figures. September, 1908 ....

Vol. 2. The Silva of California, by Willis Linn J

Other series in Botany, Economics, Engineering, En
Bulletins, Lick Observatory Publications, Mathemati
Academy of Pacific Coast History, and Zoology,

UNIVERSITY OF CALIFORNIA CHRONICLE.—A
issued quarterly, edited by a commit
year. Current volume No. XII.

ADMINISTRATIVE BULLETINS OF THE UNIVER
the Recorder of the Faculties. In
Report, the Secretary's Report, and

Address all orders, or requests for information c
The University Press, Berkeley, California.

CPSIA information can be obtained
at www.ICGtesting.com
Printed in the USA
BVHW092321201118

533618BV00021B/2174/P

9 781333 811164